# A Love

# with France

## Robert Brown

## Maps and Drawings by Robert Brown

**Memorable holiday experiences of a wine loving family in France.**

⌊ 1999 Robert Brown

Drawings by Robert Brown
Maps by Robert Brown

Published by Roban Press
Fax. 01482 632892

ISBN 0-9536614-0-7

A CIP catalogue for this book
is available from the British Library

Printed in UK by Fisk's Printers of Hull.
www.fiskprinters.co.uk

*To the Browns,*

*Anne my very best friend, and children, Robert and Cheryl, without whose encouragement this book would never have been written.*

*May the enjoyment of France, and wine, pass down to the third generation.*

*For Matthew Finn, my first grandchild.*

# A Love Affair with France by Chapter

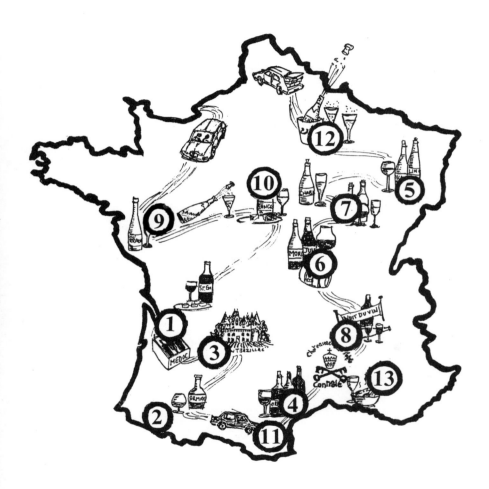

# Contents

# Introduction

'A Love Affair with France' is a collection of experiences, often humorous, of the Brown family in the pursuit of the perfect blend of unforgettable holidays and excellent affordable wine.

In this quest, over the past 20 years we have travelled throughout France and have become true Francophiles recognising France as being probably the most complete holiday country in the World, with an infinite variety of scenery, climate, people and, of course, wine!

We are not experts on wine but enthusiastic amateurs who appreciate and enjoy good quality wine. The flavour and enjoyment of which is enhanced by the memories of the tasting, the discussions with the wine producer, who is usually the vigneron, the sunny day amongst the vines, on opening a bottle at home in England in the depths of Winter. Opening a bottle of wine purchased from the local supermarket or High Street wine shop lacks this enhancement!

The wine purchased on holiday gives further pleasure in that the price you paid in France is substantially lower than the price you would pay at home, if indeed you could purchase the same wine. There are of course exceptions to the rule. At the high price level of quality wines from Bordeaux and Burgundy it is often the case that wine purchased from reputable UK wine merchants is lower in price than if purchased from the château in France. Suffice it to say, the wines the Browns drink, and those the true wine drinkers drink, do not usually fall into this category!

The changes effected by the Government abolishing Duty and increasing the volume of wine and spirits that can be brought into the UK has led to an increase in the number of people popping over to France on wine buying expeditions. This in turn has created the atmosphere for a more ambitious approach to buying wine in France.

This book will serve as a useful guide to those seeking more from buying wine in France than simply a day trip to the Channel port supermarkets, and for those people who wish to travel in, and enjoy, France.

In our 20 years of holidays in France we must acknowledge our early introduction to France by the camping company Canvas Holidays[1] and later, the gîte and auberge holiday specialists VFB[2] both of whom provide excellent bases for exploring the wines and beautiful countryside of France.

On the subject of wine, a variety of wine books have served to whet the Browns' appetite; 'Eperon's French Wine Tour'[3] especially the stories of Sablet and Pouilly-sur-Loire; 'Arlott on Wine'[4] especially his conversation with the Juliénas wine grower who bottles his wine when the moon is on the wane; and the wine catalogue 'Roger Harris Wines'[5] in which the descriptions of the cru Beaujolais villages and their sumptuous wines encouraged the Browns to make the first of many detours to this wonderful region. This beautiful and interesting region is only a few miles from the main A6 autoroute to the west of Mâcon and sadly, is missed by the majority of travellers hell bent on their blinkered drive south to the Mediterranean coast.

Finally, I hope you enjoy reading of our experiences and feel the need to enhance your enjoyment of wine by visiting *La Belle France* again and again.......

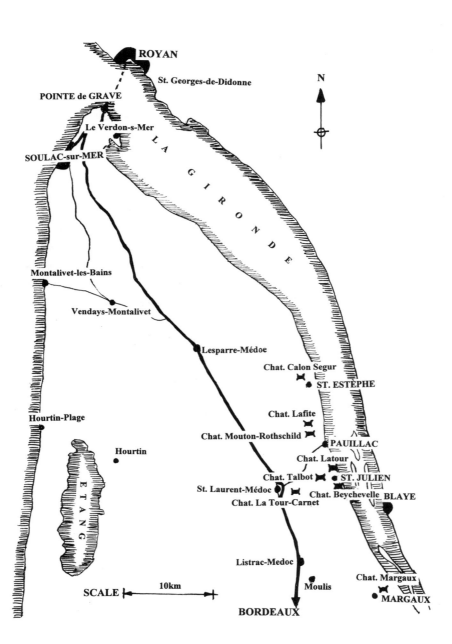

ROYAN

St. Georges-de-Didonne

N

POINTE de GRAVE

Le Verdon-s-Mer

SOULAC-sur-MER

L A   G I R O N D E

Montalivet-les-Bains

Vendays-Montalivet

Lesparre-Médoe

Chat. Calon Segur

ST. ESTÈPHE

Hourtin-Plage

Chat. Lafite

Chat. Mouton-Rothschild

PAUILLAC

Hourtin

Chat. Latour

Chat. Talbot    ST. JULIEN

St. Laurent-Médoc

Chat. Beychevelle    BLAYE

E T A N G

Chat. La Tour-Carnet

Listrac-Medoc

Chat. Margaux

SCALE    10km    Moulis    MARGAUX

BORDEAUX

# 1

# Bordeaux and Bugatti.

It is fitting that our first wine holiday in France centred on the Médoc, that relatively flat area north of the Landes and north-west of Bordeaux, the home of arguably the best wine in France, and the World.

Having spent most of our children's early years on British holidays, this holiday in the Médoc was a memorable experience, our first so far south and our first in a tent. Although a little apprehensive of the channel ferry and the drive down through France, by the time we boarded the ferry across the Gironde from Royan to Pointe de Grave we felt like we were really on holiday, mixing with happy, excited French families on their way to the seaside.

Driving down the rickety gang plank, bumping off the ferry, (mind the exhaust) we finally, after a short sandy drive, reached Soulac-sur-Mer, a busy little seaside resort on the northern tip of the Médoc. Soulac was a charming place in those days, in some respects reminiscent of a wild west shanty town. We have visited Soulac in more recent times and the resort has been modernised and improved to accommodate more visitors but we feel it has lost some of its charm in becoming more commercial. However, the quality of the wines has not changed, but more of that later.

As I mentioned earlier, this was our first holiday in a tent, with Canvas Holidays[1], one of the specialist camping holiday companies on a 4 star camp site on the southern edge of Soulac within 200 metres of the Atlantic.

The fully equipped six berth tent with double bed, part shaded by umbrella pines, with toilet block and shop facilities, was a million miles away from my experiences as a boy camping *à la ferme* by Lake Coniston in the English Lake District.

Since those early days in the 70's, the tents are now fitted with refrigerators, electric lights and in some cases with en-suite facilities. However, the coming of the 'fridge' has ruled out the visit to the 'Iceman.' The tent was supplied with a cooler box which kept food and drink cool by the use of blocks of ice which could be purchased from the site shop or from the 'Iceman' in Soulac. The visit to the 'Iceman' was an experience and the children stared in amazement as an enormous circular saw cut 1 and 2 litre blocks from a huge slab of ice. I was more taken with the part restored Bugatti which was the 'Iceman's' pride and joy. Who would have thought that the old barn down at the end of a sandy lane could have housed such a treasure.

Across the lane from the 'Iceman' was a small caveau where we purchased our first Bordeaux by the litre at ridiculously low prices. This was our first taste of regional wine in France and was judged a resounding success at the time. In hindsight, I suspect the balmy evening, the ability to eat outside without jerseys or anoraks, listening to the cicadas, enjoying succulent grilled steak with fresh salad, played a greater part in the memorable evening than the gulpable red wine. Perhaps my memory was clouded by the morning-after effects of too much red wine!

Having settled into the camping routine, of breakfast al fresco with fresh croissants and coffee, bathed in the Atlantic, felt the strength and force of the breakers on our backs, played beach tennis on the open clean sandy beaches, seen our first nudists, we set off on our first wine buying expedition.

Soulac-sur-Mer, a quaint seaside resort with timber-clad balconied properties and sandy streets had a veritable treasure house of wine, a *Maison de Produits Régionaux* which kept a comprehensive range of petits châteaux and several Grand Cru wines. Of the various wines within our price range we found a very agreeable Médoc from Château La Tour Carnet, a 4th Cru wine, and vowed we would trace the wine back to its source.

At the local supermarket, a Codec, we were surprised by the range of wines from the region, and indeed we have found that French supermarkets located in wine regions tend to supply a comprehensive range of wines from the area but only a very limited supply of other French wines or indeed foreign wines. (More recently, as is now the case in the UK, French supermarkets are beginning to stock a greater selection of wines but the wines are mainly French).

A memorable lunch of *moules marinière* with a bottle of chilled crisp dry Muscadet sur Lie, purchased from the Codec store, caused a mental note to be made for a future visit to the Muscadet region in the Loire.

Driving south in search of Château La Tour Carnet we passed signs for St Julien, Paulliac, Margaux and passed by vineyards of the truly great wine producers, Château Margaux, Château Latour, Château Beycheville. We stopped for a moment to pay homage to the greatest wine makers in the World and wondered if the Browns would ever have the finances to indulge in such luxury. One day, one day!

We finally arrived in St. Laurent and found the Château at the end of an imposing tree lined avenue and gingerly drove through the wrought iron gates up to the Château. The place appeared deserted and deathly quiet. We were about to beat a hasty retreat when suddenly out of one of the caves a tall sun-tanned muscular man appeared dressed in the traditional check shirt and blue cotton trousers and to our relief welcomed us to Château La Tour Carnet. This gentle giant was the cellarman and asked if we would like to visit the caves. Would we like to visit the caves, what a silly question! Although our understanding of French was limited, and he spoke no English, we had an interesting insight into wine manufacture.

**The Browns first château   -   La Tour Carnet.**

We were shown how the grapes were collected then passed through presses to extract the grape juice. Apparently the grapes are subjected to three pressings, the first is a gentle press which extracts the juice destined for the Grand Cru wine, a second press at a higher pressure to extract juice for Médoc wine and finally a high pressure extraction to produce wine for the workers. (Apparently each estate worker receives a free litre of wine a day, I nearly asked him for a job!) The grape juice is then fermented into wine and stored in oak barrels for a minimum of 2-years before bottling.

From his pocket he produced a strip of sulphur, which is ignited to produce sulphur dioxide, an anti-oxidant for the wine. We then walked through several caves, vast barns, where rows and rows of barrels of last year's vintage and beyond, were slowly maturing in this dark, cool, silent almost subterranean world, to be opened, tested and finally bottled at some future date, into quality wine, for future consumption.

Finally, the tasting, a fruity intense wine full of blackcurrants with hints of cedar and spices, gorgeous! I do believe the cellarman enjoyed the tasting as much as we did. We bought two cases in wooden boxes and paid 26 francs a bottle, that was in 1977.

During our meanderings through the regions of Margaux and Paulliac we visited the Cave Coopérative at Paulliac and found 'La Rose Paulliac' to be a good, fruity, easy drinking wine with less tannic taste than other recent vintage wines.

At Soulac we also experienced our first French market, stalls of salads and vegetables, fruits, cheeses, meats, sausages, and polished marble slabs covered in a hitherto unseen range of fish and shellfish, all fresh and of excellent quality. The stall holders were surrounded by jovial ruddy faced locals, greeting friends and laughing their way through the early morning. We just wandered around drinking in the atmosphere, not quite wine, but intoxicating nevertheless. We trundled back to the campsite with our purchases and in the evening declared the *champignons à la Grecque* positively ambrosial to say nothing of the fresh salad drizzled in local olive oil and wine vinegar with a hint of garlic. The seafood and the Bordeaux Sauvignon Blanc were a perfect match. Finally the nectarines, full of flavour and juice so unlike the nectarines on sale in the UK.

On our last evening in Soulac, after several games of boules, listening to the distant sounds of 'Brown Girl in the Ring' and *'Ce plan pour Moi'* we agreed that wine from La Tour Carnet was good, very good and a perfect *'au revoir'* to Soulac.

During our holiday, we purchased an assortment of château bottled wine, all of which gave pleasure on drinking and helped firm our resolve to return to France for further wine holidays. However, none could compare with the wine purchased from our first visit to a Grand Cru château. I believe it is the association of the wine with the pleasures experienced at the original visit and tasting that has been the driving force behind the Brown's regular wine holidays in France.

Eleven years later we returned to Soulac and found the resort to have undergone a face-lift with pedestrian-only areas, and the sleepy little town had become more commercialised with boutiques and craft shops. We could not find the *Maison de Produits Régionaux,* the market was still there but had been modernised. I think I preferred Soulac the way it was, or is it that time colours ones memories? During this visit, we returned to Château La Tour Carnet. There was evidence of improvements having been made to the fabric of the buildings and the gardens, and there was an air of commercialisation which we had not detected during our earlier visit. We called in the Office, were not offered a visit, and purchased wines from two vintages, now with the new label, designed to give shelf-appeal to the product. We asked why the '84 vintage, which many believe was a mediocre year for Médoc wines, was not on their price list; only to be told that they had sold the entire vintage to the French Navy! We have often wondered why the French sailors look so happy and contented at work. We purchased wine at 135 francs a bottle. On drinking the wine we did not enjoy the wine as much as our first purchases, perhaps our tastes had become more sophisticated, or the modern quality was not to our liking, or perhaps the memories of that first visit to a Grand Cru château and caves had elevated our first purchases to a thereafter unattainable level of enjoyment.

Further investigation of wine prices confirmed my suspicions, that quality wines from the Bordeaux region, especially the Grand Cru wines were often more highly priced when purchased at the château or within the region from wine merchants, than could be purchased in the UK. As lovers of affordable quality wine, we convince ourselves that the enjoyment of the wine is significantly improved, if the wine has been purchased at a bargain price!

In recent times we have tended to buy Grand Cru wines from French supermarkets, not from the Channel port supermarkets which tend to cater for the booze-cruise buyers, but from inland supermarkets with a low percentage of foreign buyers. We have found that prices can be a half and sometimes a third of the price of wine from the same château and the same vintage, when purchased in the UK.

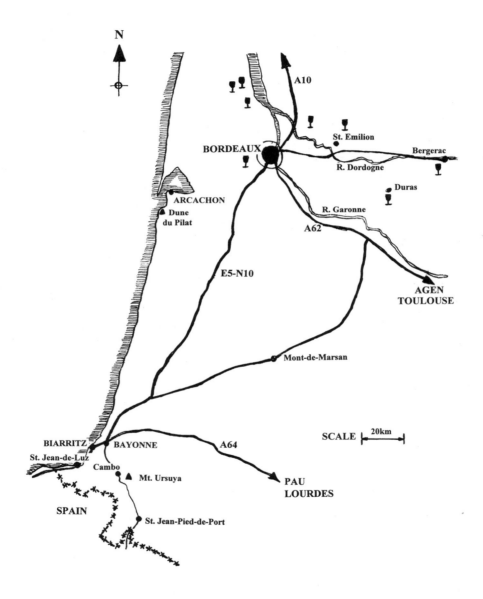

N

A10

St. Emilion

Bergerac

BORDEAUX

R. Dordogne

Duras

ARCACHON

Dune
du Pilat

R. Garonne

A62

E5-N10

AGEN
TOULOUSE

Mont-de-Marsan

SCALE 20km

BIARRITZ · BAYONNE · A64

St. Jean-de-Luz

Cambo · Mt. Ursuya

PAU
LOURDES

SPAIN

St. Jean-Pied-de-Port

# 2

# Izarra and Ilkley Moor.

South of the Médoc lies the Basque region in the foothills of the Pyrenees, and although not noted for its wines, has several fond memories for the Browns.

Travelling south from Bordeaux one crosses the Landes, a vast area of pine forest. Driving through this area one is overcome by the fragrance of the pines, it is not a sudden waft but is constant and all-enveloping with an intensity which is almost overpowering. Once experienced, never forgotten!

It is worth making a detour to climb the Dune du Pilat to the south of Arcachon, reputed to be the highest sand dune in Europe. The view across the Bassin D'Arcachon over the oyster beds to the pine forests beyond, and the view out to sea, into the Bay of Biscay, are well worth the climb. If you visit in Summer, we advise that you wear footwear as the sand can be very hot, and there is an awful amount of it to walk on if you are bare-footed! Our children commented, "Lovely sand, but too dry for sand castles!"

On to Biarritz, an established, well-heeled seaside resort made famous by visiting Royalty at the turn of the century, whose popularity has continued due to the pleasant temperate climate.

Biarritz is a complete contrast to Soulac at the northerly tip of the Landes. However five miles to the south lies St. Jean-de-Luz, a pretty fishing village and distinctly Basque, especially around the harbour. The beach at St. Jean-de-Luz is clean and well protected from the Atlantic breakers making it ideal for children. This is in contrast to the beaches at Biarritz and on the Landes coast, which are often subject to the full force of the Atlantic, where a few minutes of being subjected to body-shattering breakers are more than enough for the average holidaymaker.

The countryside inland from St. Jean-de-Luz, at Cambo-les-Bains, St. Jean-Pied-de-Port and in the surrounding hill villages is very picturesque with green hills, wooded valleys and trout-filled tumbling streams.

We found out, on our first night in the area, why the trees and meadows were so green and lush! As we approached our VFB[2] holiday gîte the air was heavy, hot and extremely humid, almost too much for the weaker sex. We had only just finished unloading the car when the storm started, thunder and lightening and rain, wow! Vertical stair-rods, we have never experienced anything like it before or since; although a storm one night when camping in Grado, Italy, again with VFB,[2] came a close second.

In the morning all was clear, the sun was shining and the oppressiveness of the previous evening was soon forgotten. That morning we walked to the top of a local hill, the 678m. Mt. Ursuya, and the view through 360 degrees was unforgettable. Northwards, to the pines of the Landes with the Bay of Biscay clearly visible until it finally merged with the horizon, east and west to the wooded hillsides and south to the Pyrenees; yet another treasured memory.

It is easy to understand why the Basques are a proud people and why they jealously guard this beautiful region. They are a passionate, colourful race who appear to have four real passions:-speaking and writing a language full of X's and J's, *fêtes* including copious amounts of food and drink, pelote in all its various forms and, most infuriating to the visitor, a passion for obliterating road signs!

The Basque region *en fête* is a sight to behold, every village seems to have a square with a *fronton*, a large high wall against which the high speed ball game of pelote is played. The square is the gathering point for the *fête* and, the main event, apart from the fireworks, is invariably a pelote tournament with substantial money prizes for the winners.

After the hard fought pelote match, which on this occasion was played with the open hand, rather than the wicker basket, interest switched, for the younger generation, to the fairground roundabouts and stalls, whilst the adults concentrated on the food and wine. As the evening progressed and the drinks flowed, the chatter of happy revellers was interrupted by the sudden appearance of a Basque band at the head of a procession of Basques dressed in colourful traditional costume. The happy chatter was soon drowned by the band, who, in their white shirts and trousers, with a brightly coloured sash as a waistband, wearing the famous traditional red berets, formed a circle and entertained the crowds with their infectious beat and Pyrenean mountain music. My daughter, at that time musically in transition, from recorder to clarinet, was particularly taken by the flute player who extracted fantastic sounds from his whistle by deft finger control, whilst holding the end of the instrument with the same hand.

While the band played, they were followed into the square by stilt-walkers from the Landes, riders on horseback and other groups in traditional costume, and finally, the 'flaming bull' was paraded around the square. This is a sight to behold, the mock bull, spitting fireworks and crackers from every part of its anatomy, showering red-hot sparks into the crowd, was cheered, or jeered, until after a few circuits, it disappeared down one of the narrow cobbled side streets. Walking through the lingering sulphurous smoke, one could be forgiven for thinking that one had just witnessed the passing of the devil from hell!

I have enthused so much about the area and the people, I have almost forgotten to mention the wine and the food, *sacré bleu*, this will not do!

First, Izarra, not a wine by any stretch of the imagination! Izarra is actually a liqueur, made from *eau de vie,* armagnac, grain fruits, honey, flowers, sugar and herbs, and is available in two colours, yellow and green, as is its more famous cousin, Chartreuse. We found it an interesting drink, and during the holiday, used it in a variety of ways:- as an aperitive, between courses as Calvados, as a liqueur with coffee, and as a morning-after restorative. We could not decide where its use would be best served. Perhaps my son's comment, that it tasted like alcoholic cough medicine, may provide the clue as to its best application. Izarra is definitely an experience! But one to be missed, perhaps not.

The wines of the region are like the people, warm, full-bodied and friendly, with no pretentions to greatness, unlike the prestigious wines of Bordeaux to the north.

Of the reds, we found Irouléguy, with its high percentage of the Tannet grape, full-bodied with a distinctive flavour, very drinkable with the local food. We also found that the local white and rosé wines were excellent with seafood and complemented the super-fresh flavours of river trout, not to mention the local cheeses.

On reflection, our enhancement of the wines was brought about by the food, the people and the countryside, which must be experienced to be appreciated. As is often stated, "Life is a series of experiences."

Seeing the children, one morning, screwing up their faces at the faint smell of silage from the freshly collected, full-cream, farm milk was certainly one of these. The smell caused my daughter to exclaim, "Wertach!" Whereupon the family collapsed in fits of laughter. All she was doing was recalling one of her memorable experiences from the time we stayed in a farmhouse bed and breakfast in Bavaria, where the animal accommodation formed the back of the farmhouse, just behind our daughter's bedroom. Who said, "All experiences are good experiences!"

Close by our hamlet, in the Basque region was a small rural restaurant, just a few covers, where one called in the morning to book a table and order one's evening meal from a selection offered by Madame. The food and wine, the atmosphere and the company in this rural restaurant, were first class, in fact so good that we visited Madame's restaurant on three successive nights. The culinary delights served by Madame were all provided at the same price on each night, but on the first night we received three courses, on the second night four courses and on the third, five courses! This begs the question, which is raised on occasions during family discussions, if we had visited the restaurant on the fourth night would we have received six courses? Perhaps we should revisit Madame's rural restaurant to find out.

During this holiday, whilst visiting the picturesque border town of St. Jean-Pied-de-Port, we crossed the border into Spain and stumbled on the French equivalent of the present day British 'booze-cruise'. The locals parked their cars in France and walked over a wooden footbridge into a duty-free haven in Spain. Sniffing a bargain, the intrepid Browns crossed the bridge, jostling with contented French returning with their weekly purchases. We bought some spirits and were fascinated with a queue of people with empty lemonade bottles, waiting to be filled with colourless liquid from a tap on the wall. Was this some special water with healing powers? A close examination showed it to be the Spanish equivalent of Cointreau, on draught! Perhaps we were right in the first place.

We shared our gîte with a French family who occupied the ground floor, and had the annoying habit of playing their radio, very loudly, from the early morning. In fact I believe the local farm cockerel used the radio as an alarm! After several days of being awakened at some unearthly hour by the radio, we decided to take action. That night, after a late enjoyable dinner on the veranda, over coffee with the lighter (40%), slightly sweeter, yellow Izarra, we decided on a sing-song. After a superb rendition of 'On Ilkley Moor' we retired to bed and slept soundly until mid-morning when we were awoken by the cockerel, he had obviously missed the radio alarm that morning too. We never heard the radio again.

On our way home, heavily laden with food and wine, we made a detour to St. Emilion, a medieval wine town, and bought a few bottles of wine, including Château Robert. (more for the ego than the contents!) After walking up and down the steep cobbled alleys, in the heat of the day, we were suddenly assaulted by the heady aromas of toasting macaroons. We immediately felt the need for food. As if destined, we found ourselves in the old square, espied a *crêperie*, and ate memorable *crêpes,* washed down with an earthenware tumbler of cider, in the dappled shade of ancient plane trees. Further memories, which served as a reminder to visit St. Emilion again.

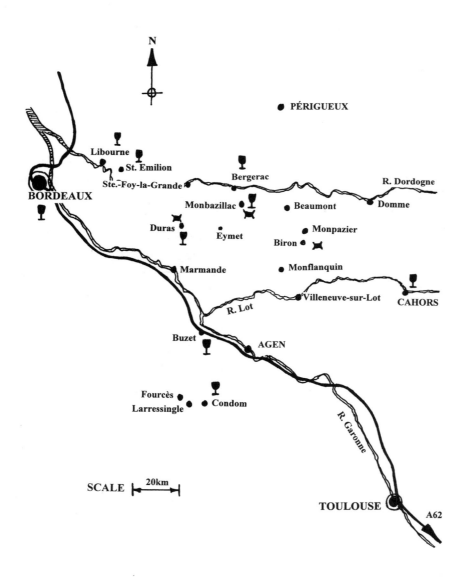

N

PÉRIGUEUX

Libourne

St. Emilion

Ste.-Foy-la-Grande

Bergerac

R. Dordogne

BORDEAUX

Monbazillac

Beaumont

Domme

Duras

Eymet

Monpazier

Biron

Marmande

Monflanquin

Villeneuve-sur-Lot

CAHORS

R. Lot

Buzet

AGEN

R. Garonne

Fourcès

Larressingle

Condom

SCALE ⊢—20km—⊣

TOULOUSE

A62

# 3

# Belle-sœ ur and Bergerac Rosé.

For lovers of the Cotswolds, and rural England, longing for a bygone age when country lanes were free of motor traffic, the gentle rolling countryside of the Dordogne is a must. To be able to picnic by the roadside in the corner of a field of poppies, amongst the rustling vines, with only the smells of the countryside, and be passed by no more than a cyclist, two motorists, the yellow post van and a farm vehicle, in an hour, is well worth the drive down from the ferry.

Of all the various climatic regions of France, this is probably the most appealing to the British, being warm in Spring and Autumn and hot, but not unbearably hot, in Summer. This is possibly the main reason for the relatively large contingent of British home owners in the region.

We start our wine holiday to the south and south-west of Bergerac in the small town of Duras, built on a ridge in the shadow of a formidable Château, which has undergone extensive rebuilding over recent years. Duras is surrounded, not only by vines, which are used to make Côtes de Duras wines, but also plum trees, whose plums are dried to make prunes and prune jam. All are specialities of the region.

The Coopérative in Duras sells quality wines under the 'Berticot' label, which surprisingly, considering the quality, has only recently appeared in Britain. The Sauvignon Blanc is fresh and fruity and is excellent chilled on a warm sunny Summer's day. The reds are good drinking wines and the best of these, which are made from the same grapes as the petit château wines of Bordeaux, would stand up well in a blind tasting. Interestingly, it is only in recent times, that the British supermarkets have discovered the wines of this region. But, we believe the wines found, tasted and purchased from the grower are generally of better quality than those offered in the local UK supermarket. Our advice to wine drinkers is simple; if you like the wine bought in the UK, you'll like the wine better in the Duras region, and it will be at a more favourable price.

One night, in Duras, at dinner, in the Hostellerie de Ducs, we selected a Côtes de Duras Cabernet Sauvignon '85 vintage, only to be brought a '89 vintage by the nattily-dressed waiter. I rejected the wine saying I had asked for an '85 not an '89. He shortly re-appeared, beaming, offering the same bottle with the vintage changed by pen to '85. I admired him for his cheek and graciously accepted the bottle. We have visited the restaurant, which serves excellent regional food, on several occasions, and we now have a good rapport with the same waiter. Would this have happened in Britain, I doubt it! We have often laughed at this, all that is necessary, is to say, "Do you remember that waiter in Duras?"

There is also an inexpensive, sparkling white, produced by the *méthode champenoise* sold in the region, which when chilled, served with fresh strawberries and *crème fraiche* is the ideal solution to lunch on a hot Summer's day, preferably without the children! With luck, the UK supermarket buyers will discover it one day.

To the east of Duras, one enters *Bastide* country. The first of these *bastides* is Eymet, which we visited on market day. Under one of the arcades surrounding this ancient square, we found a British estate agency, which served as a meeting point for the local British residents to discuss the weather and would you believe it, the fortunes of the local cricket team! We have returned to Eymet but the estate agency is no more, perhaps the return of the strong pound will bring it back! Exhausted after a heavy but successful bartering session in the market, over some glasses and porcelain, we adjourned to the nearest café for a coffee, ordered *café au lait*, and then noticed that most of the customers were also drinking large coffees. Strange, we thought, until we heard the other customers talking. We had stumbled into the second British stronghold in Eymet!

The region is ideal walking country, so one day, on a short walk, we stopped in a small hamlet for our lunch of baguette, ham, cheese and tomato plus a bottle of Côtes du Rhône, purchased from the local store. As we were finishing, we were approached by a retired Englishman, who it transpired, was resident in France, and was visiting the hamlet where he was assisting his son in the conversion an old presbytery into a holiday home and the outbuildings into a separate gîte. He invited us to join the family for coffee, with whom we spent a pleasant couple of hours. The son and his family told us that they had bought the near derelict property and were rebuilding it as part of a 10 year plan. Their ultimate objective being to retire to the area, as their parents before them. Our initial reaction was one of envy. Later that evening, we pondered whether we would be willing to spend all our holidays and all our spare time for the next 10 years, in what is admittedly a wonderful part of France, when there are so many other untapped areas of France and other wines to discover? We decided to continue with the wine holidays, until such time as we find our Shangri-La.

The whole area is so attractive to the British, gentle rolling hills, pleasant climate, uncluttered and pollution-free roads, an easy pace of life, good food, excellent wines but, alas, no British pubs! The French bar, tends to be frequented by youths playing pin-ball machines and/or by locals sat on stools at the bar, competing for conversation with the ever present corner television set which is playing and talking to deaf ears. Definitely not the place for a romantic *tête à tête*. This was brought to mind late one evening in Summer. It was just after a heavy shower, when I saw an old gentleman, in a suit, carrying a furled black umbrella, stepping gingerly through the puddles in the cobbled street. Aha! I thought, a retired 'Brit', I wonder if he, like me, misses his local.

To the north of Eymet lies the Bergerac wine region, where good honest reds and whites are produced including Monbazillac, the sweet wine of the region, which at its best, can compare favourably with its more illustrious cousin, Sauternes. Of the Bergerac wines, one of the better wines is produced at the Château La Jaubertie, owned by Henry Ryman, who with Australian influence, produces an intense rich, fruity red reserve, which can on occasions be purchased in the UK and, on our last visit to the region, from the regional products/wine shop in the main square in Domme. When we first visited La Jaubertie, we enjoyed chilled Sauvignon with its fresh, spicy fruity flavour and thought it stronger in flavour but equally as good as the softer, less intense, Sauvignon from Duras. The Australian partner, Charles Martin, then invited us to taste what, (his words not mine), "Is probably the best rosé in the world."

It was good, very good, but had he tasted Gigondas rosé from Raspail-Ay or Collioure rosé from Cellier des Templiers, I think not! But, then again, neither had we at that time! The rosé was so fruity, it was a hot, still Summer's day, sheer bliss!

Two miles to the north-west, lies the Château de Monbazillac, maker of the sweet golden nectar which competes favourably with wine from Sauternes. One could argue about the merits of Monbazillac versus Sauternes, but there is no argument, when it comes to the photogenic Château, and the view from the terrace. The panorama across the valley of the Dordogne can be savoured from the terrace café whilst partaking of a well-earned *thé au citron*.

Although excellent wine can be purchased from the Château de Monbazillac, the area is also dotted with small vineyards where hard working vignerons produce with loving care, good honest wines, at reasonable prices.

## Château de Monbazillac.

The vineyards can take some finding, simply because the French have different ideas on direction and distance to the British. Do not be dismayed if after passing a sign indicating vineyard in 300m, that after travelling 1500m you have still not found it, you will, eventually.

On one such wine tasting trip, we eventually found the vineyard, a large old sprawling farmstead with several outbuildings. The place appeared deserted, but eventually, our door knocking achieved the desired results and an old woman appeared. We explained that we would like to buy some wine and asked if this was indeed the château. She replied in the affirmative and said that she would ask her *belle-sœ ur* to attend to us. Both my son and I thought, beautiful sister, is this possible? A slightly younger woman appeared, but beautiful, she was not! We told her we would like to taste and purchase some wine, she pointed in the direction of the outbuildings and said that we should seek out her *beau-frére*. On our way across the cobbled yard, I mentioned to my wife, Anne, our disappointment, who then cleared the mystery. *Belle-sœ ur* and *beau-frére* are French for sister-in-law and brother-in-law! I was relieved to know that this was not another of the differences between the French and British!

The *beau-frére*, apologising for the dusty conditions, as he was in the middle of moving and modernising his bottling plant, ushered us into his office, for a tasting. We tasted Bergerac rouge, Bergerac sec, and his speciality, 16% Monbazillac. During the tasting, after ascertaining that we were not Dutch but English, he proudly told us that his château had been built by the English in the thirteenth century. So after all, the English did not only build *bastides!* Perhaps the British television programmers should produce a series about the British bricklayers and joiners who worked on French construction sites in the 13th century?

As I mentioned earlier, east of Duras lies the *bastide* town of Eymet, which serves as a starting point for a short tour of the *bastides*, fortified defensive towns built by the English in the thirteenth century. The tour takes in Villeréal, and the hill top village of Monflanquin, with its superb views over the Dordogne countryside. Having decided that this would be an ideal spot for a picnic, we retraced our steps into the village and returned with *baguettes, jambon persillé,* (ham aspic with parsley) *rillettes d'oie* (goose meat paste) and strawberry tarts (which only the French know how to make.) A *bon repas*!

Continuing, in a north-easterly direction one is drawn to Biron, a château village on the way to Monpazier. The château is enormous, standing head and shoulders above the surrounding countryside. Lying off the main road, it is a peaceful and reflective place, and well worth the detour.

Just the place to enjoy a pastis on the terrace of the restaurant at the foot of the château, as we did that afternoon. Not any old pastis, but Pastis de Marseille, created by Paul Ricard in 1932, the recipe which has made him probably the richest man in France. During our second Ricard, Anne asked which was my most memorable glass of pastis. Swirling the ice cubes in the fragrant opalescent beige-yellow liquid, I thought for a moment and then recounted a hot July day at a truffle fair in the Vaucluse. It was a Sunday morning, and we joined the locals in drinking *'tomate'*, an ambrosial blend of Ricard, Evian and Grenadine, very tasty with the nutty Nyons olives drizzled in oil and coated with thyme. All of which served as a useful appetiser to the speciality of the day, truffle omelette.

Anne said, her most memorable moment was one market day in Carpentras, when we were entertained as we drank at a street bar, by three excellent jazz players playing superbly, standards such as 'Sweet Sue'. It transpired that the guys were from New Orleans, and visited the south of France each Summer, busking at street markets and playing the odd 'gig' in the evening. Yes, I mused, that was indeed a memory to recall in the future.

What about the night in the garden of the chambres d'hôtes, when we lost to the French and Belgians at *boules*, and surprised the victors by offering them a choice of three pastis, that was a good night! But as the man from Marseille said, whom we met in the Haute Savoie, there is only one pastis, Ricard! We both finally agreed on the impromptu jazz concert we witnessed in Carpentras as being the most memorable.

Happy with our memories, and suitably refreshed we headed for Monpazier.

Monpazier, undoubtedly a major tourist attraction at the height of the season, but when we visited in late May, was almost deserted. It is an intensely picturesque *bastide*, especially the arcaded main square with its ancient covered market hall, and we could easily see why travel writers wax lyrical about this place. The route then takes one to Beaumont, a little disappointing after Monpazier, but with several attractive features including one of its original fortified gates, and arcades around its medieval market hall.

The Browns, being intrepid explorers, ventured further south, not only in search of *bastides*, but also to seek out the aptly named wine, Buzet, and to find the 'water of life' to the true Gascon, Armagnac. As malt whisky is to the true Scot, Armagnac is to the Gascon. We drove south, stopping in a tree-lined square of a small village, which we approached through an old castellated gateway. No sooner had we opened our flask of coffee, decaf. of course, (it is such a pleasant change from French café coffee) when in the silent square, we heard a door creak. Looking round, we saw an old man approaching. Are we parked in a restricted area? Are we blocking out his ancient lights? No, he was just an extremely friendly, inquisitive, old man, who wanted to pass the time of day. The questions flowed thick and fast. Did we like our Peugeot? who were we? where did we come from? were we on holiday? did we live in the area? had we property in the region? Relishing a good natter with the English, he proceeded to give a potted version of his life story, how he had lived in the village all his life, had a large grown-up family, and enjoyed life in his sleepy little village, extolling the virtues of the pace of life, and finally, all this was made perfect by the Armagnac! At this I became very attentive. He went on to say that he had some 54 year old Armagnac, and would we like a glass? There are usually one or two things one regrets in life, this was one of mine. As I was driving, I, on behalf of my family graciously, nay selfishly, declined his generous offer. We chatted on for a while, until, during a lull in the conversation we made our excuses, bid the old man *"Au revoir, à bientôt"* and drove off to Buzet.

Later that day I asked the price of 50 year old Armagnac at the Janneau distillery in Condom. That was when I realised I had made a mistake earlier, and would forever regret my polite refusal to the old man!

On to Buzet, to the Coopérative which, it is claimed, produces serious wine, indistinguishable from good château-bottled Bordeaux. The Coopérative by the Canal Latéral, which runs parallel to the River Garonne, no longer produced a 'cuvée Napoleon', apparently because it infringed another company's trade mark or name (at least I think that was the reason). We have since encountered a similar problem in Rasteau, where the 'Domaine de Papillons' had to change its name for similar reasons, after initially changing the name to the Provençal spelling 'Parpaïouns'. Fortunately, in both cases, the name change did not affect the quality of the wine!

The Buzet wines were savoured by all, and the Château de Gueyze was selected as the best. This wine is still drinking well over dinner on a cold winter's night back home. We have purchased Buzet wines from British supermarkets, but there is no comparison to the Château de Gueyze purchased from the Coopérative in Buzet.

After a French lunch of *pâte, baguette,* Buzet and a bowl of delicious red cherries, purchased from a village street market on route, we sat by the canal with our backs against a plane tree, enjoying the warmth of the noonday sun, as the water-life passed by at a leisurely 4 miles per hour. Discussing the episode recounted earlier when Brown senior, actually refused a drink, only firmed my resolve to continue our journey to one of the homes of Armagnac, the Janneau distillery in Condom.

South of Buzet lies Condom, straddling the River Baïse, the home town of the great Armagnac producer, Janneau. Our teenage children thought the town's name amusing, and broke out into laughter when told that the English for Baïse is Kiss!

Condom is an attractive town with an imposing cathedral on the hill with well preserved, adjoining cloisters.

We crossed the river to the House of Janneau and marvelled at the range of products and at the prices. It was here that I confirmed that a 50 year old bottle of Armagnac would cost £250; and I had refused to taste a 54 year old Armagnac, three hours ago! I felt as sick as a parrot. Still the story does bring a little merriment to the family from time to time.

**Medieval Larressingle.**

We ended the day visiting two delightful *bastides*, Larressingle and Fourcès. Larressingle a small fortified *bastide*, built as a religious stronghold, was so peaceful and quiet. In this apparently deserted medieval village one could almost feel the presence of those ancient bishops carrying out their ecclesiastical duties.

The second *bastide*, Fourcès is entered by crossing the River Auzone. Crossing the bridge, reminds one of a Monet garden scene, where the stark, well-worn, ancient walls of the château dip into, and contrast with, the circles of water-lilies on the tranquil waters of the dammed river. This *bastide* is rather unique, in that instead of being centred around a 'square' square, it is centred around a 'round' square. It is very photogenic, as can be seen in the printed photograph, 'a *bastide* in Gers' on page 94/95 in the book 'Terence Conran's France'.[6] Even though the photograph has been laterally transposed during the printing it is still a beautiful place! Yes, Fourcès is well worth a visit, to escape from the hustle and bustle and walk down the ancient alleys, through history, and finally, to the square for a well-earned coffee in one of the arcade cafés, is yet another memorable experience.

To the north-west of the region across the river Dordogne lies the medieval village of St. Emilion, the centre of the great wines of the region; the best of which compare favourably with the first growths of the Medoc. St. Emilion, to which we paid a brief visit on an earlier wine holiday, is a must for all lovers of wine. The narrow steep streets harbour many wine shops selling a comprehensive range of wines from St. Emilion, Pomerol and the surrounding districts. The village also attracts coach-loads of tourists, who after their allotted thirty minutes, can be seen scurrying down the alleys with their cartons of three bottles, and packets of macaroons, back to the coach and on to the next tourist destination.

St. Emilion should not be rushed, it is, to all wine lovers, a sacred place to be savoured. Browsing through the many wine shops, one is impressed by the range of wines, and the range of prices, from the lowly 40 franc regional wine to the 3000 franc top estate wines of Pomerol and St. Emilion. Perhaps one day, when I grow rich, I will buy a case of Château Pétrus. Well, we are all entitled to a fantasy now and then!

Walking through the various alleys, we stumbled on an actual cave, stacked with a reasonable quality, reasonably priced St. Emilion Grand Cru. Pleased with the find, we bought a case; not in the same league as Château Pétrus, but bought from the cave next door to the wine merchant who stocked Château Pétrus. Perhaps some of the latter wine's greatness will have rubbed off on our lesser wine. We can only dream! We also purchased a few bottles of a Pomerol, Château Robert! "Not only father, but now son also on ego trip," said Anne, recalling my purchase of this wine on an earlier visit.

To complete our visit, we purchased some toasted macaroons, and walked down to the village square for cider and *crêpes*, which incredibly, tasted as divine as on our previous visit to St. Emilion.

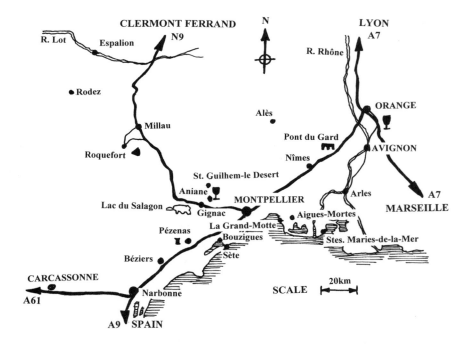

# 4

# Mince pies and Daumas Gassac.

The *Autoroute du Soleil,* follows the river Rhône south until Orange where it splits, left for the Côte d'Azur and Italy, and right for Spain. Taking the right fork, the Autoroute, now called *La Languedocienne,* passes within six miles of Châteauneuf-du-Pape, a top wine town, which we will visit on a future holiday. It continues south-west, passing two of the more prestigious Côtes du Rhône villages with their own Appellation Contrôlée, Lirac and Tavel.

For those who have an interest in Roman history, or marvel at the ingenuity of the Romans, a detour to the Pont du Gard is a must. Built by the Romans, as an aqueduct, to carry water to Nîmes, it is a wonderful feat of engineering. A photograph taken of the visitor walking across the top of the aqueduct will make a good conversation piece back home. We were surprised how narrow the Pont is at the top, and amazed, that there were no hand rails. So, if you do venture across, pick a wind-free day!

The Autoroute continues south-west, bypassing Nîmes, skirting the Camargue and onwards towards Montpellier and the Hérault region.

A visit to the Camargue is essential, as this flat delta of the Rhône is unique, offering the visitor yet another facet of this wonderful country. Where else can you find rice growing in the fields, next to sunflowers, next to vines. As one drives deeper into the Camargue, one passes the famous wild black bulls, the wild horses, the cowboys, and the flocks of pink flamingos, often no more than a shimmering pink line on the horizon. The heat haze affects one's perception of size and distance, making objects on the horizon appear nearer than they actually are, as we found out when seeking out the flocks of flamingos!

Suddenly a walled town appears, Aigues-Mortes, a remarkable place. Built in the thirteenth century, but this time by the French, as a seaport, it is now stranded 5 miles from the Mediterranean by centuries of alluvial deposits from the River Rhône. It stands as a powerful reminder to what can be achieved by team effort, in a common cause, in this case, as a seaport for launching crusades. This well preserved town, with its grid-iron arrangement of narrow streets, sits comfortably within, and hidden by, the imposing high-walled fortifications. In fact, you can walk all around the walls of this square town, taking in the Camargue panorama, and 15 towers, on route. Once the circuit has been completed a glass of the local wine, Listel, at one of the many bars in the town's main square, is really appreciated.

Continuing the drive to the sea, one passes the pink mountains, which are actually man-made piles of sea salt. The salt is collected from the *étangs* which are sectioned off into large salt pans. It is strange to see the piles of salt with a pinkish hue in contrast to the sea salt collected on the Atlantic coast near Noirmoutier, which is a sandy colour. No wonder the flamingos are such a bright pink colour feeding in these wetlands!

The area is also home to the world famous Perrier water, but as this is a wine lover's guide to France, we will dwell no further on this matter. Eventually the road reaches the Mediterranean and the purpose built seaside resort of La Grande Motte. For students of architecture, the 25 year old resort with its futuristic curved concrete apartment blocks, marinas, and umbrella pine-lined streets, is extremely attractive, and a good example of the tasteful development of an area which was, before the discovery and introduction of DDT, a mosquito-ridden lagoon.

**Holiday Apartments - La Grande Motte.**

Before turning inland to the Hérault, it is worth continuing along the coastal road, past *étangs* (lagoons) glistening in the bright sunshine, the blue vista of which is broken by the pink flecks of feeding flamingos, and the rows of cages of the shellfish farms. On reaching Sète, a large fishing town and resort, where the Canal du Rhône meets the Mediterranean, every visitor cannot fail to be attracted by the brightly coloured fishing crafts, and be seduced by the aroma of *bouillabaisse* and garlic wafting from the numerous sea-front restaurants and bistros. Lovers of good food must stop for a bowl of this delectable fish stew, with a "do-it-yourself island kit," rounds of toasted bread, *rouille* and grated cheese, washed down with a glass or two of the local dry white wine. What a way to enjoy lunch!

Driving past the Bassin du Thau, probably the largest area of shellfish farming in France, buy oysters from Bouzigues, excellent, and at reasonable prices! We noted, for a future visit, that each year Bouzigues holds an annual oyster *fête* and it was agreed, that on such a visit, the Browns would have to be accompanied by a bottle or two of good Champagne.

At Pézenas, another beautiful town with narrow arcaded streets, many too narrow for motor cars, the traveller must seek out the mince pies, made to an original recipe, using mutton, brought to France by Clive of India; excellent, either hot or cold, and written of in glowing terms, as the *petits pâtés de Pézenas*, by John Harris in his humorous book 'An Englishman in the Midi'.[7]

Driving northwards the Browns were seeking one of the best wine producers in the d'Oc, the Guiberts of Domaine de Daumas Gassac. Before leaving England, we always carry out basic research on the region, and of course the wines, and as a consequence, are well prepared to enjoy the holiday from the minute we arrive. Prior to this holiday, a comment in Hugh Johnson's 'The World Atlas of Wine',[8] in the section on Languedoc and Roussillon caught my eye. I quote, "Experience will discover the outstanding sites, as it has at the Domaine de Daumas Gassac, at Aniane, north-west of Montpellier. This domaine, on a patch of volcanic debris, is making Cabernet Sauvignon of astonishing quality." The key word to the Browns was 'astonishing' and on the basis that if one of the top wine authorities made such a comment, it must be good, we agreed it would be well worth finding.

The road to Aniane passes through Gignac, along miles of country lanes, flanked either side by rows of giant plane trees. On the long straights, and there are many of them, it is like driving through a hypnotic, stroboscopic tunnel, as the sunlight flickers through the leafy canopy of the plane trees. This is real France, bright sunshine, fresh clean air, no traffic, but sadly lacking the black-bereted Frenchman on his bicycle, with his *baguette* in his pannier. Still one cannot have everything! I could not resist taking a photograph of one of these tunnels. To obtain the best effect, and capture the symmetrical perspective, it was necessary to stand in the middle of the road; safe enough in this area, but not to be tried on the M25!

Whilst in the area we stayed a few nights in a hotel on the outskirts of Aniane. It was still very hot when we arrived, and the Browns took little time in finding the pool. Suitably refreshed, we showered, and after a long cool drink, enjoyed an excellent meal, (with local wine of course.) We did, however, notice that the restaurant served Daumas Gassac, but we decided to defer our first taste until we visited the Domaine.

Bed beckoned, but what we expected to be a good night's sleep was not to be! Our room faced due south, and the only means of ventilation was via a door, which gave direct access to the pool-side for the occupants, and direct access to the bedroom, for outsiders. To keep out the light and heat, there was a ceiling to floor roller shutter. Fearing the risk of intruders, either two or four legged, or of the slithery type, but desperate for ventilation, we left the door open and closed the roller shutter to within an inch of the ground.

It was so hot, on reflection a Turkish bath would have been more comfortable! Halfway through the night, dripping in perspiration we discovered the infamous, fleecy plastic backed bed sheet. Once this was removed, we finally enjoyed a reasonable night's sleep! This experience has set a precedence with the Browns, wherever we stay in France, the first check Anne makes on entering the bedroom is whether the bed is fitted with an 'Aniane' fleecy plastic sheet. Who said the only memories are good memories?

In the morning, suitably equipped for the day with a hearty French breakfast, we set off to find the Guiberts. We eventually found the Domaine down a twisty, dusty, side road, signposted Capion, off the Aniane to Gignac road. We were met by Mme Guibert, who invited the Browns inside for a tasting.

Just stop me, I mused! She ushered us into her tasting room, controlled at 18°C, where, at an old long wooden table, we were treated to one of the most reverent and dignified tastings imaginable.

We shared the tasting with an Austrian couple, who had purchased wine from the Domaine in the previous year. Why is it that young Austrian males sport twirled moustaches!?

The tasting was superb! We started with the slightly petulant rosé, produced from the grapes of young vines, and proceeded to the white, which was positively stunning. The white contains Chardonnay and Viognier grapes, and has a richness of citrus fruits which gives the wine a unique and elegant flavour, with a good after-taste. Experts would define the flavours more precisely, and in greater detail; suffice it for the Browns to declare the wine as excellent, and one of the most appealing whites ever tasted.

Mme Guibert proceeded to explain how she, an academic from Montpellier, and her husband, a glove manufacturer from Millau, found an area with a unique *terroir*, planted vines, and proceeded to produce their own style of wine, in an area not previously noted for quality wines. Because of its location, the wine can only be called a Vin de Pays d'Hérault, but it should not be long before Daumas Gassac is given a superior designation on merit, as it compares favourably with top quality Grand Cru Bordeaux wines.

So to the show stoppers, three vintages of rouge, all different, but each one a star in its own right. Although the wine is predominantly made from Cabernet Sauvignon, it is the smaller percentages of the other grapes, Merlot, Malbac, Syrah, Cabernet Franc, Cinsault, Carignan, Tannat and Pinot Noir which make the difference in the vintages. With such a blend, coupled with the wine makers skills, it is not surprising that the wines have such richness of fruit and depth of flavour. We could not agree on the best vintage, so surprise, surprise, we bought a case of each, in order to continue the debate at some future date.

On reflection, Hugh Johnson was correct, the Guiberts do indeed produce 'astonishing' quality wines.

These wines are now available from a limited number of UK outlets, at similar prices to the Domaine prices, which reinforces our Bordeaux experiences, that top quality wines are at similar prices, or cheaper, in the UK than in France. However, the staple diet of the amateur wine lover, the French regional wine, is still significantly cheaper in France than in the UK, if indeed it can be purchased in the UK. *"Vive La France!"*

After dinner on the second night, relaxing on the terrace after yet another excellent meal, we were suddenly jolted back to reality by loud music being ghetto-blasted from the village. From our past experience, this noise would probably continue into the small hours of the morning. On the basis that if you can't beat them, join them, we decided to visit the village. As we approached the village square, the music had a hypnotic effect and attracted people from all corners of the village, like bees to the honey pot.

It was the night of the Grand Ball, with a mobile Dance/Rock band, playing on a make-shift platform, the back of a trailer. The square was crowded with happy locals, and a few inquisitive tourists, who after a few drinks, became indistinguishable from the locals. It was a good night!

We always find it so satisfying to see four and five generations of the same family having such an enjoyable, uninhibited, happy time together. Sadly, these family occasions are becoming increasingly rare in the UK, as families move away from their roots and from close relatives. Perhaps in our fast moving society, we could learn lessons from these rural, local communities. Arriving back at the hotel, 'danced-out' we slept soundly that night.

A must for all visitors, is a visit to St. Guilhem-le-Désert. From Aniane, the road follows the River Hérault, crosses it on the Pont du Diable, through rocky garrigue country, past the commercial Grottes de Clamouse, to one of the most photogenic villages in the region, St.Guilhem-le-Désert. It is built around the Benedictine Abbey founded by William (Short Nose) Duke of Aquitaine in 800 A.D. Since 806 A.D., when William returned from Rome with a 'relic of the true cross' the village has, over the centuries, been a place of pilgrimage and consequently enjoyed the prosperity of the pilgrim trade.

**St.Guilhem-le-Désert.**

The village, nestling in a side valley, straddles a small stream, a tributary of the Hérault, and has many old stone properties and twisting alleys. In the square, in front of the Abbey, shade is provided from yet another of the wonderful plane trees, where a cool pastis, or iced drink, in one of the cafés can be appreciated. The village, in spite of the presence of many gift shops, still retains its old world character.

During our first visit to St. Guilhem-le-Désert, we purchased a Limoges plate, which had been hand-painted with a border of butterflies, by a painter from Paris, who stayed in the village during the Summer months. This plate has pride of place in our dining room, as it not only reminds us of St. Guilhem-le-Désert, but also of one of our favourite Rasteau wines, Domaine de Papillons, (which has had to change its name, but more of this later) and the famous, Papillon brand of Roquefort cheese. We have since revisited St. Guilhem-le-Désert but sadly the Parisian has moved on, but at the end of the day we have the plate and the memory.

Under time restraints, we purchased a selection of local wines, St Chinian, St. Saturin, Corbières, Minervois etc. from a local supermarket and found them to be reasonable drinking wines. As a consequence, we have made a note to return, on a future occasion, for a wider exploration of the area.

We took time off to visit Carcassonne, a walled medieval city. We were a little apprehensive, as it has been described as a poorly restored city. We are pleased to say this is not the case. The view of Carcassonne from the rest stop on the east carriageway of the Autoroute is breathtaking. From this point, and as one walks around the walls, one can easily see why the film 'Robin, Prince of Thieves' was filmed at Carcassonne, as it could quite easily be, medieval Nottingham. It tends to be well visited by tourists, but the place has adequate car parks outside the city, thereby giving good pedestrian access to the interior and the walls. We purchased an antique map of Vaucluse, an area of excellent wine and one of the Brown's favourite regions, but because it lies north of the Luberon has not yet been discovered by the masses.

Outside Carcassonne, we purchased from a supermarket, bottles of Fitou, 'Terre Natale' produced by the Coopérative in Fitou, and Fitou produced by le Pilot des Produceurs de Villeneuve-les-Corbières, these spicy deep reds have been appreciated on many a cold Winter's night, at home. We also bought *vin doux*, Rivesaltes, which is an excellent accompaniment to sweets and puddings. The Browns added Fitou and Rivesaltes to the future visit wish list.

Leaving the area, driving north west, we decided to take time out to visit the home of one of France's greatest cheeses, Roquefort. The cheese is produced in the town of Roquefort-sur-Soulzon which is located 26 km south of Millau. We would recommend a visit through the galleries carved out of the Tufa rock, which by being porous, keep the cheese at constant temperature and humidity, ideal conditions for the growth of the blue veins in the cheese.

Originally rye bread was allowed to grow mould and the mould developed the blue veining in the cheese, this has now been superseded by modern techniques where the mould is introduced into the cheese during manufacture. Our guide told us that the old wooden laths, which had been used for maturing and storing cheese for generations, would have to be replaced by plastic. Apparently, Brussels has decreed that wood is unhygienic!

We bought some cheese, rye biscuits and a bottle of Châteauneuf-du-Pape and set off to find a suitable place for lunch. We stopped in Espalion, on the river Lot, and had a very enjoyable lunch in the park by the side of the river. The cheese maker was right, Châteauneuf-du-Pape is the ideal accompaniment to Roquefort! Suitably refreshed, we decided to walk around the town, we crossed the bridge and I saw a camel tied to a lamp-post! I thought for an instant that perhaps the Roquefort had somehow reacted with the Châteauneuf-du-Pape and caused me to hallucinate!

To my relief the rest of the family had also seen the camel. The children investigated further and found it was a real life advertisement for a travelling circus which was visiting the region.

**The River Lot at Espalion.**

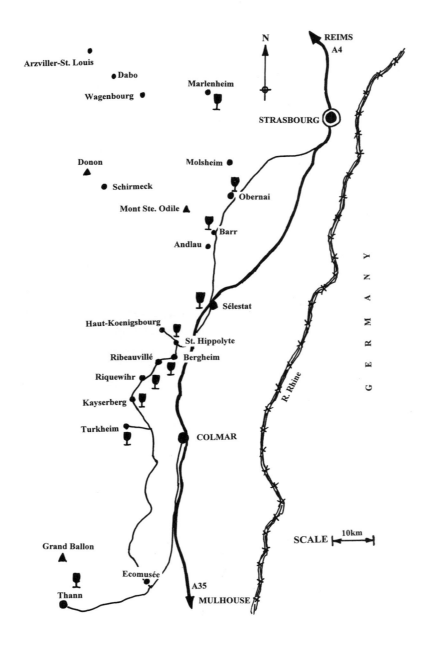

# 5

# Storks and Gerwürztraminer.

If someone had taken me blindfolded, and dropped me in the middle of an Alsatian village, in the height of Summer, then removed the blindfold, I would not have believed them, if they had told me I was in France. Germany yes, Switzerland possibly, but France never!

France is an amazing country, with such a diversity of climate, countryside, people and customs, it is easy to see why most French people prefer to holiday in France. It does indeed have everything.

This region is a complete contrast to the hot dry garrigue of the Midi, the shimmering flamingos in the Camargue, and the aromatic pines of the Landes. It is one of the prettiest regions, and has over the years been French-German-French-German and French, and, as a consequence, has adopted the best features of both countries in its food, its wine and its general ambience.

In the north of Alsace, the forested hillsides and mountains, stacks of drying timber, pretty hamlets of Alpine style chalets scattered amongst carefully manicured meadows, could convince one that this is indeed Switzerland, but the local beer, Bière d'Alsace, is a gentle reminder that this is really France. Both, my son and I, cannot understand why the Alsatian beer drank in Alsace tastes so much better than the Alsatian beer sold in French supermarkets in other regions, perhaps the beer doesn't travel, or perhaps they keep the best for local consumption! Shades of 'Black Sheep' and 'Old Peculiar' in North Yorkshire, we concluded.

For those who are mechanically minded, or canal lovers, the barge lift on the Rhine-Marne canal at Arzviller-St.Louis is a must.

Barges are raised and lowered 44 metres in 15 minutes, whereas, prior to its introduction in 1969, it required 17 locks and a full day. Boat trips on the lift and along the canal, past the scrub-covered gun emplacements, which formed part of the Maginot line, to the crystal centre of Lutzelbourg are available, if required. The Browns after a walk through the forest picking fresh blueberries, preferred to sit in the shade, by the side of the canal, eating the morning's pickings covered in *crème fraiche*, washed down with a glass or two of chilled Gerwürztraminer, to a trip on a canal boat, but wouldn't any wine lover, we ask?

The road south to Wangenbourg, one of the most 'Alpine' of the northern villages, passes through wooded hillsides to Dabo, which has a most attractive modern post office, if modern architecture is of interest to the traveller. Outside the town, perched on a hill, is a small chapel, which can be climbed for a stunning view of the northern forests of Sauverne and Walscheld. This is especially beautiful in the evening when the oblique sunlight emphasises the effect of distance in the colours of the wooded hillsides.

More sobering, is the reminder of the atrocities of war in the preserved concentration camp, high in the hills above Schirmeck, and the monument, to the poor unfortunate souls who perished at the hands of the Nazis. Standing in the camp, amongst the rows of grave stones, looking out over beautiful hilly countryside, prompts two questions How? and Why? Hopefully the European Union which has kept Europe free from war for over 50 years will prevent any repeat of the past. It is good that such places are preserved lest we forget.

It was also encouraging to see a group of English schoolchildren taking time from their mountain biking holiday to pay their respects to an earlier generation.

As a contrast to the evil of war, nearby is Mont Sainte Odile, where a hill top retreat has been built to Sainte Odile. The walk through the woods, past the spring which provides a source of holy water to the visiting pilgrims, to the simple chapel with its beautiful, intricately designed, mosaic ceiling, provides an uplifting experience.

So to the wines, the wines of Alsace are somewhat unique in being named primarily after the grape variety rather than the region. The most popular grapes used, in alphabetical order only, are Gerwürztraminer, Muscat, Pinot Blanc, Pinot Gris (often called Tokay d'Alsace), Pinot Noir, Riesling, Sylvaner and a blend of grape varieties sold as Edelzwicker. The better quality wines, produced from the Riesling, Muscat, Tokay d'Alsace and Gerwürztraminer grapes are allowed to be called Alsace Grand Cru wines. These wines are named after the vineyards and slopes, known as *lieux-dits*, and number 47 in total.

The Alsace Wine region from Marlenheim in the north, called the 'Bas Rhin' stretches south for over 60 miles, as the crow flies, to Thann in the 'Haut Rhin'. The *'route du vin'* is clearly marked, and meanders through numerous villages, all connected with the wine industry, for over 80 miles. As one drives down the Rhine plain from Strasbourg (superb cathedral and old half-timbered houses in the Petite France quarter) to Colmar, the hillsides with their patchwork quilt of vineyards remind one of the northern Beaujolais region when seen from the A6 Autoroute as one drives south near Mâcon.

The above paragraphs are more descriptive than the normal Brown style, but I believe to be necessary for the wine drinker, as he or she should know of the wide variety of wines available in this region.

Throughout Alsace, there is a strong Germanic influence with the neat, orderly, tidy, clean, newly-painted half-timbered houses, bedecked with rows and rows of window boxes overflowing with a profusion of pink and red trailing geraniums and pelargoniums, and in the attitudes of a few of the locals. The Browns encountered two of the latter, at a hotel, in the beautiful mountains in the north of the region. Dinner is served at 7.00 prompt! Late arrivals will be made to feel uncomfortable! Dinner ceases at 9.00 prompt! You must only speak to the English waitresses in French! The patron will sulk if you insist on drinking in the bar after 9.30! Who said they all went home after the war! If only a more relaxed regime existed, this hotel, with one of the best locations and views in Alsace, would be the perfect, peaceful, holiday retreat.

Fortunately, this attitude was rarely encountered during this and subsequent visits by the Browns. We found the Alsatians warm and friendly, and very helpful, especially if one spoke in French. We did however detect an initial frostiness, which disappeared when they established that we were English and not German!

The Browns had their first taste of 'real' Riesling in Barr, one of the northern 'Bas Rhin' villages. Our tasting, in one of the wine houses, started with Sylvaner, which grows well in the north, and is an easy drinking quaffing wine. It is not surprising that the locals drink this in their *winstubs*. Why is pub wine in the UK so appallingly bad, surely they would benefit by selling better quality and better kept wines? We then progressed through generic Riesling and Reserve to Grand Cru. The crispness, intensity of flavour, and depth of the grape scent with the characteristic bouquet of petrol increased and improved with the wine quality. I will never forget the petrol; in fact this is one of a handful of wines I can always pick out in a blind tasting!

Barr, like many of the Alsace wine villages is surrounded by vineyards which cascade down the gentle slopes and are only stopped from over-running the village by the small gardens and walls of the houses huddled round the main square. There are many clearly signposted walks through the vineyards with helpful signs showing the varieties of grapes and the growth from bud to mature grape. The Browns enjoy these walks during the Summer when the regimented rows of carefully tended vines with their ripening grapes follow the contours of the gentle hillsides creating mesmerising patterns of green and offer the walker attractive views of sleepy villages nestling at the foot of the carpeted hillsides. The walks enable one to start in the village and usually follow a circular route enabling the tired but contented walker to reflect over a glass or two of local wine and enjoy a *'plat de jour'* in one of the many village *winstubs*. Bliss, sheer bliss!

As one proceeds along the wine route, each village strives to outdo the previous village with its floral displays and freshly painted properties. Probably the prettiest and most visited village on the route is Riquewihr. A walled town, with ancient half timbered houses straddling cobbled streets, Riquewihr is remarkable in that in spite of widespread decimation of surrounding villages in the Second World War, it emerged relatively unscathed. Sadly it is now overrun by hordes of tourists, who snap away at the strategically placed children in national costume, and drop into the nearest wine/tourist shop for souvenirs to show to friends back home. We were surprised by the number of Americans, obviously Riquewihr is on the European tour. In spite of the tourists, Riquewihr is well worth a visit and the wine drinker should not miss a call to one of the propriétaires-négociants. We visited Dopff and Irion, and were well impressed with the useful information on grapes and wine and also with the quality of the wines, especially wine made from grapes grown on the best hillsides in Riquewihr, 'Domaines du Château de Riquewihr.' The Browns elected 'Les Murailles' Riesling top marks, but all agreed that the final choice was difficult as most of the wines were excellent, full of rich elegant flavours with long after-taste, and after 4 or 5 glasses, who cares!

On a clear day the view from the nearby hilltop castle of Haut-Kœnigsbourg stretches as far as the Black Forest in Germany and our children thought they could make out the outline of the Feldberg, the highest mountain in the Black Forest. As my son laughingly reminded me "Remember the day we climbed to the top, by mistake!" But that is another story, perhaps for a future 'A Love Affair with Germany?'

Of the villages visited, pride of place was given to Bergheim, a fortified village in the Haut-Rhin, which thanks to the main wine route bypassing the town, maintains its peaceful old world charm. Entering the village through its medieval clock tower gate, one cannot fail to be impressed by its numerous old half timbered houses and narrow alleys and the views from the ramparts with the vines on one side and the sleepy town on the other side. During one such visit to Bergheim, the village was positively throbbing, it was a *'Fête de Gerwürztraminer'!* We entered the village, only to be accosted by a pushy local asking for 10 francs for a small glass, a trifle expensive we thought but they would serve as souvenirs. In the village the main street was lined with people awaiting expectantly, for what? Suddenly, a military-type band, resplendent in buttoned blue uniforms with white trousers neatly tucked into polished black boots, and sporting tricolour cockades in their black hats could be seen approaching. They were silently marching in time, to a drum beat, at the head of a procession of brightly coloured floats, full of people in national costumes. Was this the procession on its way to the guillotine? No, thank goodness! The float occupants were laughing and shouting, a trifle tipsy, I thought, but definitely not on route to Mme Guillotine!

The floats depicted various aspects of wine manufacture, a flower bedecked float occupied by the local beauty queen brought appreciative "Oohs" from the bystanders. Other floats with locals in fancy dress, reminiscent of UK carnival floats, passed by, and finally, troubadours and walkers in fancy dress dispensing Gerwürztraminer to anyone with a glass. Getting better we thought!

Several glasses later, we joined the bystanders, who, by then were in a happy jovial mood and followed the procession through the village to the main square. The main square was crowded, and I do mean crowded. We could not believe that the sleepy little village of yesterday, where one could have heard a pin drop, could undergo such a transformation within 24 hours. The aromas from the food and drink stalls wafted across the square, and we felt like the 'Bisto kids' as we were drawn to the food as if by magnets. As we jostled in the queue, joining in light hearted banter with the locals, we were treated to an impromptu performance by a group of troubadours playing rousing gypsy music. Eat your heart out 'Gypsy Kings', we thought.

Laden with food and drink, we squeezed ourselves into the throbbing mass of happy eaters, and secured one square metre of trestle space for the Browns, where we spent an enjoyable afternoon drinking in the atmosphere, and committing to memory, snapshots and snippets of conversation for recall at some future date.

The following day it was necessary to return and purchase Gerwürztraminer from one of the best producers, Gustave Lorentz. We tasted both Riesling and Gerwürztraminer, and preferred the crisper clean flavours of the Riesling to the complex flowery mixed fruit flavours of the Gerwürztraminer. We were not offered 'Vendanges Tardives', nor their 'Selection de Grains Nobles' but at prices up to £40 per bottle I would not have bought them anyhow! However we did purchase several bottles of Grand Cru Altenbourg de Bergheim Gerwürztraminer and have found that the flavours mellow and improve with age.

In fact we opened our last bottle of '86 vintage, last Christmas, and no-one in the family correctly identified the wine. It was superb, and had developed a unique mellowness and richness of flavour. The family were divided on the wine's identity and guessed it was either a 'top notch' Riesling, albeit with a hint of Muscat, or a 'mellow' Cloudy Bay with more subtle flavours, but all were amazed, that it was a Gerwürztraminer. I knew it was a Gerwürztraminer of course, but then I had seen the label, after all it was my blind tasting! Another mental note, next time in Alsace, buy more Grand Cru Gerwürztraminer!

During our first visit to Alsace our children were disappointed not to have seen any storks in spite of seeing several nests on chimney stacks and roofs of buildings. Two years ago, we were in Southern Alsace and visited the *Eco-Musee d'Alsace*, north west of Mulhouse, which has been built on former industrial land and, surprise, surprise, almost every house in this recreated village has its own nest and resident stork. For a history of the region ( similar to the Beamish museum in Durham) and, to see real live storks, the *Eco-Musee* is well worth a visit.

Before visiting Turkheim one should make a short detour to Colmar. Although a large town, Colmar has an interesting medieval centre between the Unterlinden museum, the Tanner's quarter, and Little Venice. There are many interesting wrought iron shop signs to see in the cobbled streets, and street entertainers in national costumes. Our children were fascinated by a little old man, smaller than Granddad, who entertained the crowds whilst they listened to his organ music.

After an enjoyable al fresco lunch, on to Turkheim, the home of yet more good wine! The Grand Cru Tokay Pinot Gris from the Coopérative is very good value and excellent quality. Turkheim has many medieval buildings and three ancient gates which are visited by a lamp lighter in the Summer. Does he visit in the Winter too, or is his job seasonal, for the benefit of the tourists? We must re-visit in the Winter to check this, and at the same time call for some more wine.

Back home in England, reflecting on Alsace, we concluded that it is probably the prettiest wine region in France. The area produces a wide variety of predominantly white wines which range from the easy drinking quaffable wine bar wines to the substantial long life Grand Crus, many of which begin to reach their peak after 10-15 years. Like most wine drinkers, I doubt if the Browns will ever be able to confirm this, as wines stored at home rarely see longer than 3 years storage. Obviously a larger cellar is the answer!

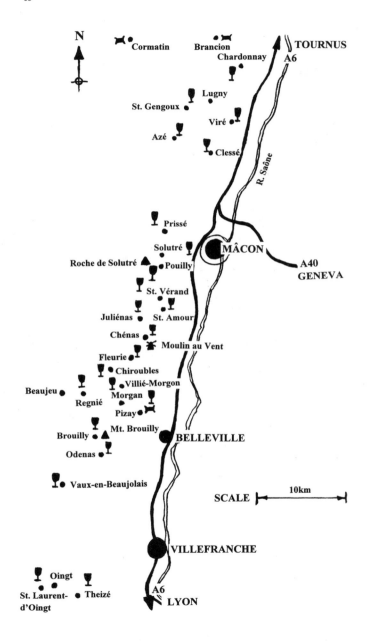

N

Cormatin

Brancion
Chardonnay

TOURNUS
A6

Lugny
St. Gengoux
Viré
Azé
Clessé

R. Saône

Prissé

Solutré
MÂCON
Roche de Solutré    Pouilly
A40
GENEVA

St. Vérand
Juliénas    St. Amour
Chénas
Moulin au Vent
Fleurie
Chiroubles
Beaujeu    Villié-Morgon
Morgan
Regnié
Pizay
Mt. Brouilly
Brouilly    BELLEVILLE
Odenas

Vaux-en-Beaujolais

SCALE    10km

VILLEFRANCHE

Oingt
St. Laurent-    Theizé
d'Oingt
A6
LYON

# 6

# Henri d'Argent and Daniel.

Our first visit to this region was as a consequence of reading a wine catalogue produced by Roger Harris[5]. His description of the wide variety of good Beaujolais wine, the wine producers and the area, prompted the Browns to dig out the Michelin maps and search for the various villages producing the Cru wines, Moulin à Vent, Fleurie, Juliénas, Chénas, Brouilly, Côte-de-Brouilly, St. Amour, Chiroubles, Morgon and Régnié. As all these wines are red, and produced from a single grape variety, the Gamay, a visit became essential. Looking at the map more closely, we found, close by, white wine villages known to produce good quality Chardonnay wines. Our mind was made up, we must go to the Beaujolais!

This area is one of the Brown's favourite wine areas, for many reasons. Firstly, the region is undulating, with many small rural villages reminding one of the Yorkshire Dales in the north, except that vines and Charollais cattle replace sheep, and in the south, the yellow sandstone villages in the vine-clad hills are reminiscent of the rural Cotswolds. Being country people at heart, the area has great appeal to the Browns. Secondly, driving, cycling, or walking through the region is like reading through the pages of a wine book. "Just like train spotting days," said Robert, "but instead of there's a 'Jubilee' or a 'Deltic,' the words are, there's a sign for Juliénas or Morgon." Thirdly, the people are so friendly and pleasant and have an enviable lay-back life style. Who wouldn't in such a magical place! There are many more reasons which will become apparent as one reads through the chapter.

The wine classification is easy to understand, there is basic Beaujolais (or Mâcon), then Beaujolais-Villages, and finally the ten superior villages which are entitled to, and proudly display, their names on the labels. These are the ten reds I have listed above.

The whites are similar, in that the basic wines are either Beaujolais Blanc or Mâcon Blanc, then Mâcon-Villages, then Mâcon named villages, such as Mâcon-Lugny, and finally those entitled to use the village name only, such as Pouilly-Fuissé and St. Véran. The grapes used are Gamay for reds and Chardonnay for whites. In addition several of the Coopératives produce a sparkling wine, the best of which are indistinguishable from lesser champagnes, these are called Crémant de Bourgogne. With such variety, one can understand why the area has such appeal to the wine drinker. There is an added bonus, the wines are, in the main, inexpensive, although the classier whites such as Pouilly-Fuissé are on the expensive side. A further bonus is that the wines, even the ten Cru reds, can be drunk within two to three years although some will be in peak condition in ten years as their northern neighbours in Burgundy. As a point of interest, red burgundies which will be discussed in a later chapter, are made from the Pinot Noir grape yet the village which gave its name to the grape used in the Beaujolais, Gamay, is located in the Burgundy region.

As I mentioned in the Introduction, this beautiful and interesting region is only a few miles from the A6 autoroute and is sadly missed by the majority of travellers hell bent on their blinkered drive south to the Mediterranean. The area stretches inland from the west bank of the River Saône for approx. 8 miles, and south from the village of Chardonnay (a few miles south of Tournus) for 45 miles, to the north-west of Lyon.

We have visited the region many times, from one night stop-overs, on route south, or on return to England, and for short breaks, and never tire of the Beaujolais countryside, its people or its wine.

**Rural Beaujolais - Vineyards near Theizé.**

Being regular visitors we have had several memorable and humorous experiences, some of which are recounted below.

On probably our first stopover, we stayed on a camp site with Canvas Holidays[1], and being weary and hungry travellers, after a refreshing shower, set out to find food. Looking on the map we noted a village, Gibles, and beyond it a town, La Clayette. Having driven many miles that day we decided to stop at the first acceptable eatery, which happened to be the 'Hôtel Moderne' in Gibles. It was a Saturday night, the restaurant was full but they had room for the Browns, great! The patron managed to squeeze the Browns into a full dining room on the end of a long table with a party of happy French people, who it transpired were on holiday and were camped in the next town, La Clayette.

We ordered 'Kirs', white wine with crême de Cassis, and sat back to 'earwig' on the conversation. Several of the diners were from Lyon on a long weekend holiday and were obviously determined to enjoy themselves, as we later found out! We ordered our meal, frogs legs for Mum and Dad, terrine for the children, to be followed by entrecôte steak with *gratin dauphinois*, and a carafe, or two, of house red. Ordering frogs legs had obviously impressed the other diners and it wasn't long before we were invited to join in their conversation.

The elected spokesman for the Lyonnais was a Mike Harding look-alike, who spoke some English, but like the one and only Mike Harding was also funny with it! The patron appeared with the sizzling starter, we were wished *"Bon Appétit"* by 'Mike Harding' who then drifted back into intense conversation with his friends. The frogs legs were superb, and the garlic and herb butter sauce, out of this world, especially when soaked up with the crispy bread. The children enjoyed their terrine as well, but I'm sure I caught one or two envious looks. The house red, Beaujolais, was pleasant, fresh and fruity, and the first carafe had disappeared before we received our main course. The steak, *saignant* (rare) was delicious, and by the time the crême caramel arrived the Browns were on almost equal footing in the contentment stakes with the French although slightly behind in the alcohol stakes!

Over coffee we noticed that the French were playing a

touching/singing game, which usually ended in peals of laughter. Being naturally inquisitive, and with eager-to-learn children, we asked 'Mike Harding' to explain. He said it was simple, all you had to do was sing the song and touch parts of your face and anatomy, but what he did not say, was that, if you fluffed your lines or your actions, you had to buy a carafe of wine. It was only when we started:- touch your head, touch your nose, touch your mouth, touch your chin, touch your chest that we realised at what point the song would end and why people suddenly fell apart laughing. The sing song cost me three carafes, but what a good night! It still creates a laugh in our house, "Remember Mike Harding?" is sufficient. It was interesting to watch one of the televised episodes of 'A Year in Provence' in which the actor John Thaw became involved in a similar sing-song but it lacked the spontaneity of that night in Gibles.

Having been woken early the following morning by the noisy munching of fattening Charollais in the adjoining meadow, we decided we had sufficient time, for a whistle-stop tour of several of the villages, before tackling the Autoroute northwards. Looking at the map we decided we should visit Villié-Morgon, Fleurie and Juliénas.

First stop Villié-Morgon, we parked in the main square and noticed that at regular intervals by the side of the road were Christmas trees, decorated with coloured ribbons and bows! We left the square and saw that the trees lined both sides of the main road through the village. Obviously, they celebrate Christmas for longer than the British we thought, but in the middle of Summer? There were people standing in groups by the side of the road, so being nosy, we asked why the Christmas trees, only to be told that today was the annual cycle race and the village was decorated for the occasion. We have visited many villages throughout France, since our visit to Villié-Morgon. Every time we see Christmas trees, we look round for the cyclists, because sure as eggs are eggs, the village will be staging its own version of the *'Tour de France.'*

After the cyclists passed we crossed the road, walked through a mini zoo, to a large imposing building, the Château de Foncrenne, on whose front wall was a discrete sign *'Dégustation,'* and an arrow pointing down to the basement. Bingo! The first room, on entering the basement, resembled an English bar but instead of dispensing beer, the waiter was offering tastings of Morgon, which were free provided one bought a few bottles. The rich full fruit flavours of cherries and strawberries could easily be detected and made for a very drinkable wine. Whilst Anne and I debated whether the Morgon, 'Cuvée de Py', from the slopes of the Mont de Py, was worth the premium compared to the Morgon and whether the ruby coloured 8 year old Morgon on special offer, had peaked, the children had found other interesting rooms in the basement.

Having agreed to purchase a selection, and to continue the debate back home, we followed the children past the cabinets displaying old wine making equipment, past a display of the range of bottles used for wine, from a 10cl. bottle up to one which I'm sure could hold 45 gallons, into the tasting hall. It was so quiet and cool, so this is one of the places were the various growers bring their wine to worship at their regular tastings.

On a subsequent birthday I was presented with a *tastevin* on a red ribbon, "Just like the ones worn around the necks of the men in the photographs," said the children. I can now have my own tastings!

On leaving the basement there was a large photograph of the Villié-Morgon football team, and they were dressed in red shirts and white shorts, Manchester United? Willy Morgan? No, the football team was Villié-Morgon!

Driving through the country lanes, almost every house offers wine to taste and buy. Should we stop and buy, but which one should we buy? We decided to continue with our original plan and visit the Coopérative in Fleurie. In less than 3 miles, we reached the next village, Fleurie, and almost fell over the Coopérative, stopped the car and walked right in.

The tasting room resembled the one in Villié-Morgon, and we were soon enjoying the fruity bouquet of the romantic sounding Fleurie. We all agreed the wine and particularly the 'Cuvée de President,' was very drinkable and could probably be drunk earlier than Morgon, (a point that should be borne in mind by the wine drinker with limited cellar space). It was surprising, although there are only three miles between the two villages, and the Gamay grape is used in both Crus, that the wines were very different in bouquet and taste. A further 2 cases of wine were somehow squeezed into the boot and we gingerly set off for our final stop Juliénas.

There was a small street market that day, in the square in Fleurie, and Cheryl pointed out the garlic stall and wondered if 'Jules Caesar' was there, as our last garlic stall market trader, in Provence, resplendent with laurel wreath had convinced the children that his name really was Jules Caesar! No, he wasn't there. We drove past the Café de Sports (more of this later) and after 5 miles reached Juliénas.

Looking for the Coopérative (Bois de la Salle) we passed an old church, offering wine tastings, but, as time was pressing, resisted the urge to stop and vowed to investigate during our next visit. We found the Coopérative, a large Château, and walked through the ornate oak double doors into the tasting room. On this occasion the tasting bar resembled a bank counter, but instead of notice boards showing currency exchange rates, details of the quantity prices of their 3 wines Beaujolais-Villages, Juliénas, and Saint Amour, were prominently displayed. If Fleurie sounded romantic, I must definitely taste the Saint Amour! We recognised the labels of the first two wines, as being similar to labels on wine purchased from 'Roger Harris Wines,'[5] and decided that the Browns should have their third tasting of the day. The Beaujolais-Villages was a rich purple colour, full of Summer fruits, and needed no further time in bottle, the ideal warm Summer evening wine.

The Juliénas had a fuller more sophisticated flavour and would probably benefit from a further two to three years in bottle. The Saint Amour was similar to the Juliénas but had something extra, or was it the name that was clouding the issue, perhaps it should have been a blind tasting! Unable to decide on one wine to purchase, we elected to buy six of each, after agreeing that the front passenger would share the foot space with a carton of wine. The car was pointed in the direction of the Autoroute, and with a cry of "Home James" we left the Beaujolais vowing to return at the next available opportunity.

Before our second visit to the region, I had purchased a superb wine From 'Roger Harris Wines,'[5], a Juliénas, produced by Ernest Aujas. I had also read of this wine in 'Arlott on Wine'[4], where John Arlott writes in glowing terms of Ernest Aujas, who refused to bottle his wine "except when the wind was in the north and the moon on the wane." It was however his last sentence in the passage, which had the greatest effect on me "It is a Beaujolais experience to have tasted it." Although the book was published in 1986, the original article had been written in October 1978, and I wondered if I would ever be able to meet M. Aujas. Later we saw a television programme in which John Arlott met Ernest Aujas in the Café de Sports in Fleurie and talked at length of wine and his special Juliénas! Our minds were made up we must find and meet Ernest Aujas.

We visited the Café de Sports in Fleurie and were told to ask for Ernest Aujas in Juliénas. In the centre of Juliénas, there is a wine shop in the form of a barrel, where the equally rotund Henri, sells his own Juliénas, surely he would know. We tasted and purchased some wine, in those days Henri used sealing wax rather than foil to cover the corked bottle. (A method of closure which is of little use to the wine drinker in a hurry, as I have never found a fast alternative to the slow process of carefully chipping off the wax, with the inherent risks of scattering red wax everywhere and bottle breakage.) We tried to pay by credit card, but Henri was insistent *"d'argent!"*

even though the card swipe machine was clearly visible, so from that day the Browns refer to him as Henri d'Argent. We asked Henri if he knew the whereabouts of Ernest Aujas but either we had a language/communication problem, or being less charitable, perhaps Henri simply didn't want to tell us.

We asked a couple of people in the street but again drew a blank. We visited the church selling wine, the temple of Bacchus, and bought some bottles, more for the racy label than the contents, and again failed to find directions. Armed with the IGN 1:25,000 Carte Topographique we set off on our own but there are so many side roads in this beautiful hilly countryside, we were unable to find the vineyard. Reluctantly we left Juliénas, but were doubly determined to find the Aujas's property on our next visit.

We did indeed find Ernest Aujas's property, but sadly, Ernest had died earlier that year. We have since made twice yearly visits to the Beaujolais and have many happy experiences of tasting various vintages with Madame Aujas and Daniel, the son, who continues to produce nectar by the barrel, just like his father before him.

As a surprise for my 50th birthday the family took me to Beaujolais for the weekend and we visited Madame Ernest Aujas and Daniel, and as a further surprise Anne had arranged a magnum of their 1983 for me. I still have that magnum and intend to drink it when I reach 57, because as the sign in the Aujas's cave states:-

### *Moyenne de la Vie Humane*

| | |
|:---:|:---:|
| *57 ans* | *70 ans* |
| *pour un* | *pour un* |
| *buveur d'eau* | *buveur du vin* |

### *À vous de choisir!*

Sadly, Madame Aujas is no longer with us, but rest assured the skills of the father have all been passed on to the son.  As a break with tradition, Daniel now produces a second Juliénas, from old vines, and given a few years in bottle, should prove a real winner. We have over the years introduced several of our friends to Daniel and all have enjoyed the experience and the wine.

The vineyards in Juliénas, as in most of the region are now more clearly, but discretely, signposted and the wine drinker visiting the area for the first time should have no difficulty in finding individual vineyards, in enjoying the people, the countryside and of course the wine.

As a base for exploring the region, a stay at the Château de Pizay, will take some beating.  To be pampered, in beautiful surroundings, to walk through the topiaried gardens on a warm Summer's evening, after a most enjoyable meal, is almost as close to paradise as a human could expect.  The key word is almost, but one evening I do believe I was as near to perfect paradise as one could be.  We had driven down from the Alsace, the temperature signs on the Autoroute had flashed up 38 degrees, we arrived almost melting!  After a swim, a shower, a gin and tonic in our air-conditioned room, we stepped out into the heat of the early evening, and, after a short walk through the gardens, decided that we should go to dinner.

The windows of the restaurant were fully open and this helped reduce the room temperature to tolerable levels.  During a most enjoyable meal, amongst the cheeses we selected was a Livarot. The waiter efficiently and expertly served the cheese until he came to the uncut round Livarot.  As if to remind the diner as to the real temperature, the cheese, when cut, collapsed and the runny cheese centre covered the plate.  This is the closest we have been to solar-toasted camembert, but the flavour was superb!  We took coffee outside, the balmy evening, the indigo-purple sky, the fresh coffee, the brandy and the intensely flavoured chocolate coated candied fruits.  I closed my eyes, yes I was in paradise!

On another earlier occasion, we had difficulty in understanding the word *'rognons'* on the menu, and without a dictionary, we asked the waitress to explain. She said she could not speak English and proceeded to draw a small bean. Not wishing to appear ignorant, we thought, if we have to eat vegetarian, so be it. When the course arrived it wasn't a mixture of pulses but a richly-sauced casserole of lamb's kidneys. The meal was excellent. Since that time we have always carried a small dictionary discretely hidden, but available to avoid any potential embarrassment in future. Needless to say we have never needed it!

Château de Pizay has an extensive range of cru Beaujolais wines on the menu, many of which can be obtained locally. The Château grows and produces an interesting range of wines including a 'Cuvée de Py' Morgon, a Beaujolais Blanc, a Beaujolais Rose and a Régnié, which are not only on sale to hotel guests, but can be purchased from the gatehouse.

There are other things to be enjoyed in this region. Inland from the vineyards, in the more hilly regions, the vineyards give way to lush meadows where birds sing, butterflies flutter by and the famous white Charollais cattle noisily munch their way from daybreak to sunset. We stopped to watch a newly born calf take its first steps, but decided to move on when the minder cow, probably the young calf's aunt, took exception to our presence. Next, we saw a goat with part of a fence stuck round its neck, perhaps we should do something about it we thought. We then noticed other goats similarly attired with wooden collars, and then the penny dropped, it must be the mating season and the wooden collars were to prevent the goats from damaging themselves during rutting.

Walking down the traffic-free lanes, through meadows of waist-high buttercups, is very relaxing. A short pause at the local bakers for fresh *baguette*, to the local store for a couple of slices of ham, a piece of cheese, and a bottle of Beaujolais, into the bar for a 'kir', then off to find a picnic spot in the shade, is a welcome break from the hustle and bustle of modern life.

Having heard so much about the quality of Charollais beef it seemed a good idea to visit Charolles on market day. Around lunch-time and feeling hungry we followed the farmers and market traders into a busy restaurant and ordered and enjoyed the French equivalent of boiled beef and carrots with mashed potatoes. Apart from the accent this could have been market day in England. The beef was good, but better than Aberdeen Angus, I don't think so!

Enough of these digressions, the serious wine drinker will have gathered that I have only mentioned 5 of the Beaujolais crus. To the north of Juliénas lie the villages of St. Amour and St. Vérand, where there are many producers of the seductive sounding St. Amour and a good value Chardonnay, St. Véran. On our travels we have found the grower, Jean Curial, affectionately referred to by the Browns as JC, produces both a long lasting St. Amour and a dry buttery Chardonnay, St Véran, which at its best stands up well against its more expensive, more fashionable neighbour, Pouilly-Fuissé. JC also produces a Mâcon Rosé, which, when drunk young, is a very good picnic wine.

Between Juliénas and Fleurie lie the vineyards of Chénas and Moulin à Vent. The Cave du Château de Chénas is the Coopérative and they have one of the largest cellars in the Beaujolais and it is well worth a visit. They supply Beaujolais-Villages, Chénas, sometimes a medal-winning Chénas, and Moulin à Vent. I particularly like the Chénas, preferring it to some of the fuller Beaujolais Crus, but that is my choice, not the family's choice. After all the world would be a pretty dull place if we all had identical tastes!

Moulin à Vent is claimed to possess great ageing potential and this has no doubt contributed to its reputation as one of the best of the Beaujolais Crus. Whether one would agree with this is down to the individual. It has a floral spicy bouquet, a ripe fruit flavour and good lasting qualities, a good wine. The old one-sailed windmill tells the visitor that one is in the Moulin à Vent vineyard.

To the south-east of Fleurie at an altitude of 400 metres lies Chiroubles, the village which gives its name to one of the lighter Beaujolais Crus. The wine has a flowery bouquet and a fruitiness similar to good honest Beaujolais but with more subtle and longer lasting flavours. Reputed to be shorter lived than other Crus, the Coopérative wine is still drinking well after five years.

To the south-east of Villié-Morgon lies the latest village to gain Cru status Régnié. We have visited the village twice and on both occasions in the middle of a cycle race. The wine is good drinking wine with more berry fruits than the established Crus; in fact more like a good Beaujolais-Villages wine. Obviously the Browns will have to investigate further!

South of the main Belleville-Beaujeu road the countryside is dominated by Mont Brouilly which gives its name to the remaining Crus Beaujolais, Brouilly and Côte de Brouilly. Brouilly is the largest and highest yielding of the Beaujolais Crus, whilst Côte de Brouilly is produced only from vines growing on the steep, well-exposed slopes of Mont Brouilly. Both wines, like all the Beaujolais Crus are good drinking wines, Brouilly being deep ruby coloured with a bouquet of soft berry fruits and Côte de Brouilly, violet coloured with a bouquet of flowers in addition to the ever present berry fruits. Comparing the two wines at various caves, our opinion is that the Côte de Brouilly has a more sophisticated and subtle flavour, and a longer after-taste. The Browns particularly enjoy the wines produced at Château Thivin, by the family of Claude Geoffray, who devoted his life to the wines and vineyards of the Beaujolais. I recall a recent visit to Château Thivin, where our tasting was interrupted by a Canadian couple who had read of the wine in Robert Parker's 'The Wine Buyers Guide'[9] and asked before tasting, the price, and then, if there was a discount for three bottles!

I could not believe it, they had broken the golden rule:- greet the wine grower, taste the wine, discuss the wine, and finally ask the price. As for asking for a discount, on three bottles, forget it! Our experience is that if you purchase one or two cases, the wine seller will usually give you a *petit cadeau*, a bottle of wine or a glass, but to ask for a discount, really!

At the top of Mont Brouilly is a picnic area with good views over the Beaujolais region, an ideal spot to enjoy a lunch of ham, fresh bread, ripe nectarines and a bottle of Côte de Brouilly. On a hot day, even in May, the gentle breeze is greatly appreciated. Close to the picnic area is a small church which is unattended but always open and the visitor is invited to buy and light a candle and reflect on life, loved ones and the peace of the World. Taking time to reflect in the quiet stillness of the vigneron's church is a moving experience.

South of Mont Brouilly, quantity takes over from quality. The near villages produce Beaujolais-Villages but as one travels south through the region, the percentage of Beaujolais increases to 100%. Driving south one can feel the warmth which is reflected in the warmer colours of the houses and the vibrancy of the inexpensive fruity purple wine, Beaujolais, produced for drinking, not storing. However, not all the wines are short lived, some can last 5-10 years.

On holiday in Collioure, (yet another wine region), I was given a bottle of Beaujolais-Villages, by a man from Lyon, who claimed it as being one of the best from the Beaujolais. During dinner in the hotel it transpired that his wife, a lassie from Liverpool, had actually worked for and met President Clinton, when he visited Lyon. This prompted Anne to recall meeting Jane Torvill in the toilets at Lyon Airport. Over liqueurs, we concluded that Lyon is obviously the place to meet people! Returning home, I kept the wine for 6 months to settle before opening it and was surprised to find it very drinkable, of excellent flavour, and nowhere near its peak. The wine was 8 years old! I will seek out the vigneron to confirm the claim of the man from Lyon, that he produces one of the best Beaujolais-Villages wines, before I make further comment.

Probably the most visited village in the southern Beaujolais is Vaux-en-Beaujolais, which many believe to be the village in the 'Clochemerle' stories by the author Gabriel Chevallier, and although the village urinal does overlook the church, it is of modern design, and anyone looking for an ornate iron *pissoir* will be disappointed. On reflection the French do seem to have a preoccupation with bodily functions, *pissoir*, or *pissotiere*, is self explanatory. The French word for the common flower dandelion is *pissenlit*, which always brings a titter to young language students. There is also a Beaujolais Pisse-Dru which is usually sold with an explanation of the origin of the name. I hasten to add that the contents of the bottle are very drinkable! There is a pleasant spot in Vaux-en-Beaujolais, by the *boules* area, with extensive views across the Vauxonne valley, where one can enjoy a light lunch of bread and cheese and a bottle of good honest Beaujolais purchased from the Cave de Clochemerle.

There are many pretty villages nearby in this region of 'Pierres Dorées' which refers to the warm golden colour of the local stone. If one can imagine the English Cotswolds, with lazy, balmy sunshine, and vines, without traffic, you will have been transported to this lovely area. We particularly enjoy walking around Theizé, the views from quaint Oingt and the very gulpable purple nectar from the Coopérative in Saint-Laurent-D'Oingt. This quality Beaujolais is produced from grapes, grown in the hillside vineyards, surrounding the villages of Sainte-Paule, Oingt and Saint-Laurent-D'Oingt.

Rather than dwell further on this wonderful area, we would suggest that wine drinker should visit, and find his, or her, own piece of wonderland!

Earlier in the chapter, the white wines of the Beaujolais were mentioned, and are now discussed further. To find these wines one has to retrace ones steps back through the wine book, through the Beaujolais villages, and the Cru villages, to the border of the *Départements* of Rhône and Saône-et-Loire. In the main the white wines are produced in the north of the region and as with the Gamay wines, the variation in flavour and bouquet one finds in wines made predominantly from one grape, the Chardonnay, is remarkable. In our wanderings in this pretty region we have used the village of Chardonnay as the northern limit of the Brown's Beaujolais, otherwise in our quest to find the northern limits of Chardonnay wines we would have had to travel through the Chalonnais, Burgundy, Chablis and Champagne regions.

Chardonnay village like the adjacent villages of Lugny, Viré, Azé, Clessé and St. Gengoux produce Mâcon, Mâcon-Villages, and, for their quality wines, are allowed to affix the name of the village e.g. Mâcon-Viré. Some of the larger Coopératives also produce a range of sparkling wines, Crémant de Bourgogne, the best of which compare favourably to some of the lesser Champagnes, with the added bonus, to the wine drinker with an eye on cost, of being a third of the price!

For the first time visitor, we would suggest a visit to either the Coopératives of Lugny or Viré where the range of Chardonnay wines and various Crémants can be tasted and compared. The Cave de Lugny, which also serves as the chais of the nearby village of St. Gengoux, has an impressive modern tasting room and is obviously one of the more successful Coopératives in the region. The basic wine is Mâcon Blanc, which is good value for money, as witness the number of French people purchasing wine in bulk and buying labels for their own domestic bottling.

There is a definite improvement in depth of flavour as one progresses through the Mâcon-Villages Blanc to the Mâcon-Lugny and Mâcon-St. Gengoux with the sharpness giving way to the buttery characteristic of the Chardonnay. This butter taste is far more subtle than that associated with New World wines and we believe has more appeal to the discerning palate. The cave also produces selected blends such as 'Les Charmes' which can be purchased in several UK supermarkets, sometimes they do get it right! The Browns preferred the Mâcon-St. Gengoux 'Cuvee Henri Boulay' with a slightly less buttery taste, but agreed to purchase a selection for further debate back home. The range of Crémant de Bourgogne from Lugny, is very good and has been discovered, to their credit, by the UK supermarkets. These wines offer a very acceptable alternative to Champagne, but in our opinion Crémant de Bourgogne produced in the Caves De Bailly near Auxerre is slightly superior to the Lugny, but more of this later. The Cave de Lugny also produces a Mâcon-Rouge, made from the Gamay grape which, although resembling Beaujolais, does not have the intense fruity appeal; a Bourgogne Passe-Tout-Grains which is a blend of Gamay and Pinot Noir, (in our opinion the blending of the fruity Gamay with the body of the Pinot Noir was a trifle disappointing) and, a Bourgogne Pinot Noir with a distinct flavour which will provide sufficient interest to the wine drinker to warrant a future trip to explore the real home of Pinot Noir wines, the Burgundy region.

Having gained a taste for the Chardonnay wines, one should then compare wines produced from old vines with wines from young vines, and the Coopérative in Viré is worth a visit. If time permits, visits should be made to individual growers, such as the accordion playing Jean-Noël Chaland in Viré who produces an excellent Mâcon-Viré 'Les Chazelles.'

Whilst the memory of good Chardonnay from the Mâcon villages is still with the wine lover, a detour to arguably the home of the best Chardonnay in the region, the area encompassing the villages of Pouilly, Fuissé, Loché, Vinzelles and Solutré should be made. This area is dominated by the Roche de Solutré, where in ancient times, early man drove herds of wild animals over the edge of the steep cliffs, presumably for food.

Of these wines, Pouilly-Fuissé is the most sought after, and as a consequence, is the most expensive, but the wine drinker, now well acquainted with the area, and its people, should seek out the lesser known, but we believe equally superb, Pouilly-Vinzelles.  If the best, of the Mâcon village wines, are four star wines then these must be five star wines.  Whether these Chardonnays are the best in France can only be resolved by visits to Burgundy and Chablis, which I will cover later.  It is the Brown's intention one day to carry out a blind tasting of French Chardonnays, and agree, by committee, on which Chardonnay to quote the lines of a famous song is 'Simply the Best.'

The region is not only of interest to wine drinkers, but to people interested in the religious history of the region.  The tourist information centre in Mâcon has several leaflets on the major churches, and suggested tours of the Beaujolais countryside, to take in the various styles of churches.  Visits should also be made to Cluny, an ancient religious town, still dominated by the relics of its once famous and powerful Benedictine Abbey, to Tournus, with its majestic Romanesque Abbey-Church of St. Philibert, to Brancion, a hill village dominated by a partially restored castle, with superb views over the valley from the grounds of the 12th century church, and to Chapaize, with its ancient belfry.

For lovers of art and quality workmanship the painted ceiling panels in the moated château at Cormatin should be visited.  For the person wishing to make a longer detour, the Museum at Château-Chinon to the north-west is a must.  The Browns stumbled on this by accident, searching one day for the home of that well-known brand of ironware, 'Le Creuset', we visited the town of Le Creusot, but failed to realise they had different spellings.  We later found that the ironware factory shop is actually in northern France, near St. Quentin.

Slightly disappointed, we drove on, past rows of poplars infested with mistletoe (who said mistletoe is usually found on apple trees, certainly not so in this area of France), to Château-Chinon, where Président Mitterand had been mayor for several years.  In the town, we found a modern museum, built in celebration of Président Mitterand's seventh year in office, containing many of the gifts presented to the Président during his travels around the world and during visits to France, by dignitaries from other countries. It was fascinating, and contained numerous examples of the skills of modern craftsmen and serves as a useful reminder that the skills of yesteryear are still being practised, around the world, in the 20th century. We were surprised how few visitors there were.

**Typical village church viewed from Brancion.**

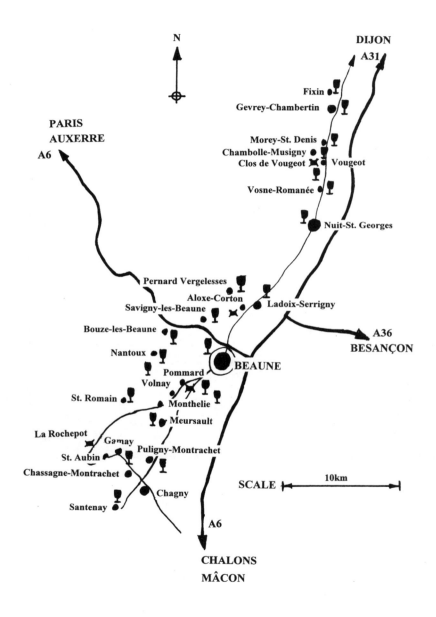

N

DIJON
A31

PARIS
AUXERRE

A6

Fixin
Gevrey-Chambertin

Morey-St. Denis
Chambolle-Musigny
Clos de Vougeot    Vougeot

Vosne-Romanée

Nuit-St. Georges

Pernard Vergelesses
Aloxe-Corton
Savigny-les-Beaune          Ladoix-Serrigny
Bouze-les-Beaune
A36
BESANÇON
Nantoux
BEAUNE
Pommard
Volnay
St. Romain
Monthelie
Meursault
La Rochepot
Gamay
Puligny-Montrachet
St. Aubin
Chassagne-Montrachet
Chagny
Santenay

SCALE ┣━━━━━━ 10km ━━━━━━┫

A6

CHALONS
MÂCON

# 7

# Reine Claude and Corton.

$A$s our first visit to Burgundy was as an addition to a visit to the Beaujolais, it is right that this chapter follows the chapter on the Beaujolais.

This short visit, a specific search for Pommard, was prompted by an earlier period in my working life, when away from home for a time, my colleagues and I found solace in the evenings in good food and wine. After extensively sampling the hotel wine list, invariably the wine we returned to was Pommard, because it was very good, and as I recall, relatively inexpensive at the time. Since that time, Burgundy wines have enjoyed considerable success, and inevitably, as demand exceeds supply, the prices rocket to a level outside the pockets of the average wine drinker. The purpose of the visit was therefore twofold, to check that the memorable Pommard was still memorable and to check if it was affordable to the wine drinker.

Driving north from the Beaujolais, because of time restrictions, we deliberately turned off the Autoroute at Beaune, thereby avoiding distractions such as Mersault and Puligny Montrachet. By skirting Beaune we were able to visit the small village of Pommard without the temptation to linger in what is arguably the best Chardonnay region in the World. On entering Pommard there is a large walled vineyard which belongs to the Château de Pommard, just the place to carry out my short survey. With apprehension we drove down the drive, parked amongst the Mercedes and BMWs, paid our 20 francs, and joined the short queue for the tour. Dressed casually in shorts and jeans, next to a well heeled Swiss quartet, one felt a trifle under-dressed, but the next visitors were in similar attire to the Browns, so we relaxed, but the Swiss looked slightly uncomfortable. The tour guide arrived and led the small party into a cobbled courtyard and down steep stairs into the cellars. The cellars with inter-connecting rooms and corridors, were actually underneath the courtyard. We were given a very informative insight into Pommard and its production. The guide extolled the virtues of the Pinot Noir, a more sophisticated grape than the simple Gamay of the Beaujolais, (his words not mine) and went on at length to explain the presence of the dirty black mould which not only covered the walls, the barrels and the bottles but I believe would have enveloped the Browns had we stayed in the cellar much longer! None of the bottles were labelled as the all-encompassing mould would have attacked the paper labels. The guide said that the bottles were washed and labelled as required and reassured the visitors that the cellarman would label the wine correctly! After walking past barrel after barrel, and thousands and thousands of carefully stacked bottles, I did a quick mental check and estimated the total value at being several millions pounds. Who would have thought that underneath the quiet cobbled courtyard was a veritable Fort Knox of wine! It is no wonder that producers such as these have resorted to overseas investment to survive.

Finally to the tasting, but only one glass! As the tasting was in the cellar, we were first instructed on warming the glass, then, on why laying the cork horizontally across the top of the opened bottle allowed air to pass the cork and enhance the flavour of the wine (but apparently not necessary for less sophisticated wine.) Next he poured the wine into glasses, and advised the party on how to hold the glass in the candle-light to check the wine colour. (As the guide was obviously into his sales pitch, would he have given the visitors anything but a colour-perfect wine, I mused!)

He then instructed us on how to hold the glass by the base and swirl the wine to allow the rich aromas to be released, and finally allowed the party to taste the wine. The wine was very good and as memorable as in my distant hotel days. The tour guide apologised for the wine being a little on the cool side, so why didn't he hold the tasting at ground level in a warmer room! So to the sales room, £20 plus a bottle, and older vintages significantly more expensive. No-one, not even the well heeled Swiss, who were over for a formal wine tasting in Beaune, purchased any wine. So my short visit confirmed yes, Pommard was a memorable wine but no, it was not affordable to the average wine drinker, at least not from the Château de Pommard!

We did purchase a few bottles of Côte de Beaune-Villages and Côte de Nuits-Villages on the approaches to Beaune but found them to be disappointing, when compared back home, to good Beaujolais Cru purchased at less than half the price.

We have visited the region more recently in search of good Pinot Noir at affordable prices, with more success.

To the wine loving layman whose quest is to find quality wines at affordable prices, the Burgundy region is far more complicated than its southern neighbour, the Beaujolais. There are excellent vineyards which are often subdivided and produce wines of differing quality, from ordinary to brilliant, without any obvious reason for the differences. The skills of the grape grower and the wine producer are of paramount importance in Burgundy and the quality is reflected in the price. There is one other factor that affects price and that is hype/demand. The price of a particular vintage is usually dictated by the demands, or indifference, of the American buyers. Reading books by the experts on Burgundian red and white wines, there is a common agreement on the best wines, but at affordable levels, the reader is left in a bewildered and confused state.

The Browns when confronted with the problem of how to find good value quality wine, found the solution. Staying in a pleasant rural B&B, after breakfast, in conversation with Monsieur and Madame, we discussed our main reason for visiting the area, our quest for good wine. At this Monsieur became very interested and when asked if he could point the Browns in the right direction he excused himself, and returned with his hand-written 'Shoppers guide to Burgundy'. Eureka! The answer to my prayers! On reflection, in our own way, we were following the practise of many wine importers, who rely on recommendations by word of mouth, in producing their wine lists. So our advice to the wine drinker is, seek out a friendly enthusiastic wine drinking Burgundian. After all if he doesn't know good value for money wine, who does! We were not disappointed.

On this visit we limited ourselves to his recommendations on producers in southern Burgundy, vowing to visit producers in northern Burgundy on a future occasion.

Our first port of call was the local village winemaker, who like most viticulteurs/producteurs, has small portions of vineyards in different regions, and as a consequence, is able to offer a comprehensive range of wines. This viticulteur offered Aligoté, Côte de Nuits, Hautes-Côtes de Nuits red and white, Hautes-Côtes de Beaune red and white, and Ladoix Premier Cru. We enjoyed the tasting and, unlike our earlier visit to Pommard, did not have to pay for the *dégustation*.

Being lovers of 'Kir', chilled Aligoté flavoured with crème de cassis, and being in Burgundy, the home of 'Kir', we purchased Aligoté to drink back home before dinner flavoured with our quality crème de cassis which we had purchased in Dijon. (Whilst in Dijon don't forget the mustard, even though most of the mustard seeds are imported, the superior flavour is all in the recipe!)

I digress, back to the wine; we were at the stage of deciding which of the wines we had to limit ourselves too, when the jovial postman arrived. He greeted Madame with the mail, wished us well with our tasting, then reluctantly departed. Before he had left the cave Madame called him back, for a glass of wine. Suddenly we had a happy 'postie'! Just the job for me I said to Anne, where do I apply! We purchased one case more than planned, yet another overloaded car, thought Anne.

That evening we ate in a village grill/restaurant, where the patron grilled meat in the dining room over an open fire. We had ribs of beef, on the bone, one large rib steak each, and a simple salad washed down with copious quantities of nine year old Patrick Hudelot's Hautes-Côte de Nuits (which when I checked in the morning was one of the wine producers on Monsieur's list!) A satisfying end to our first day in Burgundy.

The following day we rose early, and refreshed with hot croissants and coffee, set off on our mini tour. We passed through Bouze-les-Beaune (an interesting name!) only to find the viticulteur, who reputedly sells excellent Bourgogne red at 23 francs a bottle, was out. We were more successful in Nantoux, where I, at last, found reasonably priced Pommard. We tasted Hautes-Côte de Beaune, Pommard and Monthélie, an interesting comparison, and preferred the beefier Pommard to the lighter more fragrant Monthélie. Across the square an empty café was for sale. Savouring the Pommard, an idea formed, we could purchase the café and convert it into an English tea room with a wine bar selling gulpable Pommard.

Just an idea! Happy at last with my case of Pommard we set off to find Monsieur's source of white Burgundy.

We passed through Pommard, past the Château de Pommard, through Volnay, Mersault, Puligny-Montrachet, to St. Aubin. If driving through the cru villages of the Beaujolais is likened to passing through the pages of a wine book, then this short drive is like passing through the pages of the 'unattainable white wine book'. Just before St. Aubin, is the village of Gamay, which gave its name to the grape now almost exclusively grown in the Beaujolais, but which was widely used in the wines of this area before Pinot Noir.

In the sleepy village of Gamay, next to St. Aubin, we soon found Monsieur's favourite supplier of white Burgundy but the propriétaire was out working in the vineyards, however we did meet his charming bride-to-be, who gave us a short tour of the cave before commencing on the serious matter of tasting quality white Burgundy.

We tasted two St. Aubin Premier Crus, Chassagne-Monrachet, Puligny-Monrachet Premier Cru and Mersault-Blagny Premier Cru. We voted this as our best ever Chardonnay tasting to date, and agreed that these wines should be in the Browns blind tasting session of Chardonnay wines alongside the best of the Mâconnais, St. Véran, Pouilly Fuissé and Chablis wines. We lingered over the wines and preferred the Puligny-Monrachet with the Mersault-Blagny a close second; but what quality, and at 105 francs a bottle!

The taste and flavour of the Puligny-Monrachet was sublime, not only did it have the deceptive dryness, but also a subtle butter and honey flavour, which combined with the hint of melons, and its toasty, spicy, vanilla creaminess, continued into a long aftertaste. Excellent! Certainly a wine that is a complete meal in itself. Our enjoyment was obvious to Mademoiselle, who promptly gave us the opened bottles for our lunch, and a 5% discount!

We also tasted and purchased red St Aubin Premier Cru, not as beefy as Pommard, but with finer fruitiness and greater subtlety, a wine that should drink well at five to eight years from vintage, if we can resist the temptation for that long!

With one of the bottles of opened wine, (the second we drank with *gambas,* al fresco, in our favourite village of Sablet) we purchased bread, light creamy camembert and peaches, and drove a couple of miles into the deserted countryside for a picnic. We remembered the lunch not only because of the wine, which was simply divine, but because that day was Black Saturday, the day that 7,000,000 vehicles were on the roads of France and the roads would be log-jammed. We were only ten miles from the main Autoroute, but, from our picnic point, just off the road, we counted two cyclists, an auto-cyclist, two cars, and three tractors in a 45 minute period. Perhaps that was heavy traffic for the country road!

In the afternoon we visited Beaune, and seeing the high prices of quality wines in the numerous wine shops, felt positively smug with our purchases. We marvelled at the lacquered roof tiles of the Hôtel-Dieu, and given more time would have joined the organised tour. We were amazed at the number of tourists, it is obviously a popular staging post on the coach run. We also found the Hôtel des Ducs, which houses a wine museum and made a mental note to visit, should we encounter a rainy day, on a future visit. Taking coffee in one of the pedestrianised alleys, we were treated to an impromptu concert by a band of young musicians. Beautiful music, good company, hot smooth dark coffee, if I had had a copy of 'Le Figaro' I could have passed for a native!

Earlier, I mentioned a wine called Ladoix, that night in the restaurant of the Logis de France in Ladoix-Serrigny, we enjoyed a superb inexpensive meal and a bottle of Ladoix Premier Cru from Domaine Capitain-Gagnerot. It was very good. Surprise, surprise, it also appeared on Monsieur's wine list!

In the morning we returned to seek out the Domaine Capitain-Gagnerot, but at first searched in vain. We drove back and forth through Ladoix and finally after asking directions, found it, at number 38, which although on the main road through the village has only a small nameplate discretely positioned on the open gateway as a means of identification. We drove slowly down the short drive to the courtyard in front of the cave.

We entered Reception and rang the bell, a tall middle-aged man appeared in a green laboratory coat wearing shorts, no socks and trainers. He wore spectacles and had a large expanse of bald head. If one can envisage a cross between Sergeant Bilko and Max Wall then you can understand how I could hardly contain myself. If, in his green coat, he had walked like Max Wall, I would have wet myself! We said that we would like to taste his wines, whereupon he bellowed *"Papa!"* and disappeared. Shortly afterwards his father appeared, M. Capitain, and on mentioning that his Domaine had been recommended to us by 'Monsieur', his attitude changed and we were welcomed downstairs into his cellars.

We stood by an upturned barrel, and M. Capitain disappeared, to return with several bottles. His son was similarly entertaining two French wine merchants on the next upturned barrel. We started with Ladoix, not bad, then, after M. Capitain had discarded a bottle because it was slightly corked (although I would have drunk it) a Ladoix Premier Cru, better, then on to Aloxe-Corton Premier Cru, very good. At this point his son decided that his tasters should also try the Aloxe-Corton Premier Cru, and around this time we noticed that his son, who had previously discarded the contents of his glass, had started to drink all the contents. Father then produced an earlier vintage Aloxe-Corton Premier Cru which was even better. He then said we could taste the best wine in his cellar and produced a bottle of 1991 Corton Grand Cru. Yes, we had found the best red Burgundy to date, it was truly wonderful, less meaty than Pommard but with intense lasting flavours. Out of the corner of my eye I noticed that the son was busy filling his glass for the second time.

After thanking M. Capitain for a wonderful opportunity to taste his excellent wines we ordered a couple of mixed cases and paid 105 francs for Aloxe-Corton Premier Cru and 190 francs for Corton Grand Cru, and left his cave to return later that day to pick up the wine. When we returned we were met by both M. and Mme Capitain who between them packed the wine, and made out the invoice. Typical of all women Mme checked the invoice and turned to Anne and groaned *"Oh, les hommes!"* (apparently M. had failed to calculate and write down the TVA figure), this is obviously a cardinal sin. We thanked them for their kindness and hospitality and drove off, leaving them grumbling at each other.

The following morning, we thanked Monsieur for all his help, and said that we were en route to Vaucluse, but would return to England via Champagne, whereupon he produced the name and address of his favourite contact in Champagne. Yes, networking really works!   As a parting gift, Monsieur gave us a basket of home-grown 'Reine Claude', a variety of greengage, they were delicious, and much sweeter than the same variety, subsequently purchased from a supermarket.

Having purchased Aloxe-Corton Premier Cru and Corton Grand Cru, it was only fitting that we visit the village and admire the Château de Corton-André, an extremely photogenic building with its roof of yellow lacquered tiles, and definitely one for the album.

**Château de Corton-André.**

Leaving the Côte de Beaune region we meandered north through the vineyards of the Grand Crus of the Côte de Nuits, passing through Nuits-St. Georges, Vosne-Romanée, Vougeot, Chambolle-

Musigny, Morey-St. Denis, Gevrey-Chambertin, Fixin, Marsannay-la-Côte to Dijon, a total distance of less than 30 kms. If the area south of Beaune is the route of 'the unattainable white wine book' then this is 'the unattainable red wine book!

Having said that, we stopped to marvel at the Clos de Vougeot, the walled vineyard originally owned by Cistercian monks. The vineyard is now split up between 80 owners, but where should I go to buy my case of Vougeot? I recalled the words of Jim Ainsworth from his book 'Red Wine Guide',[10] "The chances of landing on the right spot and walking out with a good bottle of wine are not just slim - they are positively anorexic," and decided that further research would be required before the Browns would make a purchase.

Out of interest I referred to Monsieur's list, and noticed that he recommended a vigneron in Morey-St. Denis for Morey, Vougeot and Chambolle. Resisting the temptation, because of time and weight restraints, we continued our journey to the Vaucluse region vowing to return and continue our tour of the Côte d'Or at a later date.

The Burgundy region also encompasses the wine region of Chablis to the north west, which extends from Chablis and its environs across the Autoroute to the villages around Auxerre. This region is not the most northerly point for the Chardonnay grape, that honour goes to the Champagne region, but it is usually considered the most northerly point for still Chardonnay wines. Chablis wines are at the opposite end of the scale to the fatter buttery flavoured Mâcon wines, producing thinner, greener wines with fresh apple and spring flavours when young, which soften with time. The subtle use of oak and the minerals in the soil, coupled with the skills of the wine maker are apparent in the higher quality wines. A fresh acidic young Chablis is the ideal accompaniment to fresh oysters, although this would be challenged by the oyster eaters on the Atlantic coast.

For a first Chablis tasting we would recommend a visit to the Coopérative in Chablis, 'La Chablisienne'. If you wish to taste

Chablis before leaving for France one of the major High street stores sells a good Chablis from 'La Chablisienne'. In the Coopérative one can taste the complete range from the humble Aligoté, through Bourgogne Blanc, Petit Chablis, Chablis, Chablis Premiers Crus to the best, the Chablis Grand Crus. Being wine drinkers although appreciating the undoubted quality of the Grand Crus, we settled for Premier Cru as value for money. As the sign in our friend's cave in Beaujolais states *"À vous de choisir!"*

Once having identified the distinctive Chablis flavour, there are many small producers within Chablis and the adjoining villages to explore. As a guide perhaps one should seek out 'a man who knows' as we did in the Côte de Beaune region!

On one visit to Chablis we stayed in Auxerre, an interesting town steeped in history, and one night enjoyed a memorable dinner, with seriously excellent *escargots*, made all the more memorable because on settling the hotel bill, we hadn't been charged for the meal! Unfortunately this does not happen often, in fact if anything there is a tendency to overcharge, so if the error is in one's favour why worry! *C'est la vie!*

A small quantity of red wine is produced from Pinot Noir, in the adjoining villages, especially Irancy, where the lightness of the wine is given more body by the inclusion of a lesser known grape, the César. Although interesting, it does not have the appeal of the Hauts-Côtes wines of the Côte d'Or.

South of Auxerre the wine drinker should visit the village of St. Bris-le-Vineux, whose vignerons produce an inexpensive Sauvignon Blanc, Sauvignon St. Bris, which is best described as a soft Sancerre, but in our experience does not have the keeping power of Sancerre, but is this not what the average wine drinker wants! The village is riddled with underground cellars and good Chablis can also be purchased here.

Talking of cellars, drive the extra four kilometres to Bailly, and visit the Caves de Bailly. The entrance to the caves is a tunnel, where you are advised to turn on your headlights and drive in. After a couple of hundred yards, when you can see the lights from a large semicircular bar, park your car. You are now in the cave of probably the best Crémant de Bourgogne producer in France. The first time we visited, it was overcast and raining when we drove in, and a bright sunny day when we emerged, this must be the best place to visit on a rainy day! We have told our friends of this cave, and having visited in cars and camper vans, they have returned, amazed at the cave and at the quality and range of the Crémants on offer. The brand 'Meurgis' is very good, and offers a serious challenge to many champagnes, but more of this in Chapter 12. Well worth a visit!

A picnic lunch in this peaceful quiet countryside, by the still waters of the River Yonne with a bottle of 'Meurgis' is to be recommended.

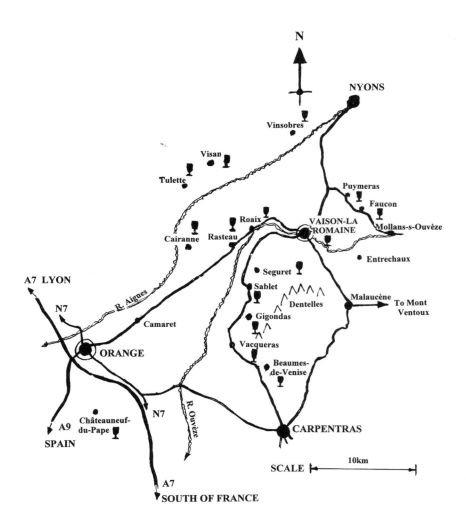

# 8

# Nuit du Vin and Pizza.

For the wine drinker the Côtes du Rhône area is a must. Like the Beaujolais region to the north, good quality gulpable wines are available in quantity, and of equal importance, available at realistic prices. As I have mentioned before, France is a complete country for holidays, and this region, and in particular the Vaucluse and the Luberon, certainly contribute to this completeness. Of all the regions visited by the Browns in the search of good wine, *joie de vie,* food and atmosphere, Vaucluse in late Spring to early Autumn takes some beating. The Luberon is as picturesque, and well liked by second-home owners, but in our opinion lacks the atmosphere, and more importantly, the wines of the Vaucluse.

One cannot write about the Côtes du Rhône wines without first reference to the greatest, Châteauneuf-du-Pape. It was at Châteauneuf-du-Pape, in 1923, that a wine classification system was introduced which formed the basis of the Appellation Contrôlée classification.

The town with its unusual name of Châteauneuf-du-Pape, was so named in the 14th century, when the Pope, at that time resident in the Papal palace in Avignon, sought a location away from the city, and built a Summer palace there. It not only served as a Summer palace but served as one of a protective ring of castles around Avignon. The Papacy had moved to France under the French Pope of the day, who, obviously knowing his wines, picked the Côtes du Rhône area for his palaces. However within a little over 60 years, the Papacy had moved back to Rome, but the vineyards in the vicinity remained. Now, all that remains of the Summer palace, is an imposing wall and tower which, from its elevated position, dominates the area, and offers the visitor a pleasant place for a picnic and good views down the Rhône valley, and across the plain to Mont Ventoux, at 1900 metres, an easily recognised landmark to the east.

One of the distinguishing features of Mont Ventoux is the military/telecommunications towers on the summit. Once, when at the viewpoint on the ramparts, in the old town of Vaison-la-Romaine, we overheard, a loud, cultured-voiced Englishman, who had been looking through his binoculars, inform his wife, and anyone else within 25 metres earshot, that there were statues on the mountain top! We hadn't the heart to tell him. If time permits, the interested visitor should drive, or if fit, cycle to the top of Mont Ventoux, from Malaucène. The views from the top, on a clear day are superb. On the road to Sault, one passes the memorial stone to the British cyclist Tommy Simpson who died of exhaustion, on the descent, in the days when the climb over Mont Ventoux formed part of the *Tour de France*. In July and August the breeze from the valley fills the air with distinctive perfume of lavender from the fields and the distilleries which surround Sault.

I digress, back to the serious business of wine. Châteauneuf-du-Pape, is the 'king' of wines in this region, and it is only right that I should start with this wine before leading on to the lesser 'royals' of the area.

In complete contrast to the Alsace where individual grape types define the wines, in Châteauneuf-du-Pape, up to 13 different grape varieties can be used in producing these alcoholic blockbusters, with a minimum alcohol content of 12.5% (the highest minimum level of any wine in France.) As a consequence the flavours are complex and intense, and with the variety of grapes available to the wine producer, the wines can be made for early drinking or for long ageing. The ground in the vineyards is covered with large rounded pebbles which act as heat sinks, releasing the heat absorbed in the day to the vines at night, which many believe contributes to the intense flavours of these wines. The stony ground certainly makes hoeing weeds difficult!

As wine drinkers, we would suggest a walk round the village of Châteauneuf-du-Pape tasting wine from the numerous suppliers, followed by a wine taster's assessment meeting, ideally over lunch, before purchase. On such an occasion we made a limited selection including wine from Paul Jeune, a name which our daughter always remembers because of the British pop singer. For one so young, (no pun intended), not a bad choice, his wine is an excellent example of a powerful, chewy, high Grenache content wine which is very drinkable within 3 to 5 years, although in a good vintage is still improving at 10 years.

Whilst in Châteauneuf-du-Pape one should visit the home of arguably the best producer of Châteauneuf-du-Pape, Château de Beaucastel, which is located to the north of Châteauneuf-du-Pape, outside the village of Courthézon. These wines are long-lived, complexly flavoured and are simply, top class wines. The down side is that they are also expensive, but even the wine drinker is allowed to indulge in one expensive purchase per visit, and opening a wooden case of Beaucastel, to carefully remove one bottle, or two, for a special meal with family or friends, is very satisfying. If on the other hand, you only wish to purchase the odd bottle, you may find as we did on one occasion, that a regional Coopérative has a limited stock at slightly lower prices than buying from the Château. On this occasion I reconciled myself to the fact that without buying from the Château I wouldn't have had the wooden box!

As wine drinkers we would only advise buying Châteauneuf-du-Pape supplied in the distinctive embossed bottles. No matter what it says on the label, unless it is supplied in the right bottle, there is a distinct possibility that it won't be true Châteauneuf-du-Pape.

The majority of Châteauneuf-du-Pape wine is red but a small quantity (2%) of white is also produced, which can vary from being light and fruity when young to a rounded and nutty flavour with age. To the Browns, white Châteauneuf-du-Pape is more of an expensive novelty, and less favoured, than some of the inexpensive Côtes du Rhône white wines.

To the north and east of Châteauneuf-du-Pape lie the pretenders to the throne, Gigondas and Vacqueyras, and the Côtes du Rhône villages of Beaumes-de-Venise, Sablet, Séguret, Roaix, Cairanne, Rasteau, Visan, Vinsobres, St. Maurice-s-Eygues, Valréas, Rousset-les-Vignes, and St. Pantaléon-les-Vignes. This is definitely paradise for the wine drinker in search of good quality drinking wine.

Leaving the Autoroute at Orange drive north east, skirting the walled village of Camaret with its clock-towered gateway, and continue along the flat valley of the Aigues and Ouveze rivers, tributaries of the mighty Rhône, into the heart of the Côtes du Rhône wine region. Miles and miles of vineyard, interspersed with the odd cypress, standing as sentinels guarding the vines but all leaning, as if in allegiance, towards Avignon, bent by the strength of the Mistral as it blows down from the Alps, and on down the Rhône Valley, to the Mediterranean. Fortunately in Spring and Summer the vines grow, the grapes ripen and are harvested before the worst of the Mistral arrives. Apparently when the Mistral blows it is non-stop for either 1, 3 or 7 days and can have a depressive effect on people. Stories abound of higher suicide rates etc.

As one crosses the plain, to the south lie the villages of Beaumes-de-Venise, Vacqueyras and Gigondas, visible against the rugged edges of the Dentelles de Montmirail, and, as one continues, past the hill villages of Sablet, Cairanne, Séguret and Rasteau, to Vaison-la-Romaine. On a star lit night, during a drive across the plain in the inky darkness, the lights of these scattered small villages take on the appearance of ships at sea, a most unusual effect, and a fitting end to a glorious evening performance of 'Turandot' at the Roman theatre in Orange. Even at night this place is special!

Undoubtedly the greatest red wine in the area, after Châteauneuf-du-Pape, is Gigondas. This wine, produced with the skills of the vignerons around the small village of Gigondas, can, at its best, compare favourably with Châteauneuf-du-Pape, in both strength and complexity of flavour. This is not surprising as the same grapes are permitted in Gigondas as are used in Châteauneuf-du-Pape. The main advantage to the wine drinker is that the price one pays for Gigondas is often substantially less than one would pay for Châteauneuf-du-Pape.

One of the best features of this village, nestling at the foot of the lace-edged Dentelles, is the small *caveau* in the village square, which is a must for the wine drinker in a hurry. In this one place, can be tasted Gigondas from all the producers in the area, and purchased at the same price as one would purchase the wine from the vigneron direct. It does, however, tend to attract British visitors, a little like flies around a jam pot! However, if one ignores those who spend an inordinate length of time pontificating with their travelling companions before agreeing to purchase one bottle, and then paying by Access, this *caveau* serves as a useful tasting room before visiting the vigneron direct. On one such visit to the vigneron, Raspail-Ay, we were fortunate to discover not only a cracking red Gigondas but a stunning Gigondas rosé. As I mentioned earlier in Chapter 3, the Australian wine-maker at Château de la Jaubertie, near Bergerac, had obviously not tasted this rosé when he claimed his rosé as probably the best. We would rate Raspail-Ay rosé as simply better!

Gigondas also has a quality restaurant 'Les Florets' where the wine drinker can, in pleasant and romantic surroundings, combine two of life's greatest pleasures, excellent regional food and vintage Gigondas from a remarkable, extensive wine list. During one visit the lavender and rosemary flavoured crême brulée was out of this world! We are always impressed with the welcome of the owners, who never fail to remember our last visit, even though it might have been over 12 months earlier. Visiting this year, father was on holiday and son was in charge. I introduced myself, *"J'ai reservé un table pour deux personnes, votre nom est Brown"*. Whereupon he answered with a grin, *"Non, mon nom est Bernard, votre nom est Brown!"* Grammatically corrected, we enjoyed yet another memorable meal.

Vacqueyras, like Gigondas, has the distinction of being a cut above the Côtes du Rhône Villages wines, in being allowed, since 1990, to use the sole name Vacqueyras on its labels. Its wines have a rich peppery flavour, and at their best are indistinguishable from their neighbour, Gigondas. It is thought of as being slightly inferior to Gigondas and as a result is less expensive than Gigondas. However our experience is that quality Vacqueyras is good value for money and outshines some of the lesser Gigondas wines. Apart from the top vignerons, good wines can be tasted and purchased from the Coopérative under the 'Troubadour' label.

The remaining villages I mentioned earlier, with Laudun, Chuslan and St. Gervais, (which are all located on the west bank of the river Rhône around the town of Bagnols-s-Cèze), form the 16 classified villages which are allowed to call themselves Côtes du Rhône Villages wines, and affix the name of the village on the label. Below this classification are the many villages which produce Côtes du Rhône wines but which can, if they meet more stringent quality levels, market Côtes du Rhône Villages wines. Even at this level the wine growers are intensely proud of their wines and the Côtes du Rhône Villages wines from the Coopératives in Puyméras and Villedieu are examples of quality wines and offer very good value for money.

Our first real experience of Côtes du Rhône Villages wine was in Rasteau, a village more known for its *vin doux* wines than its reds. Rasteau *vin doux* is the definitive port-type wine to drizzle over the local melons, delicious! However Rasteau also produces a very drinkable red wine and over the years this has become, along with Juliénas, the Brown's house red.

It was the *'Nuit du Vin'* which first attracted the Browns to Rasteau wines. This wine festival is held in August when the local vignerons close off the village and hold their night of wine. Visitors are welcomed, persuaded to purchase an engraved Rasteau glass for a nominal fee, (10 francs on our first night of wine and 15 francs on our later visits) and allowed to enter the square. Around the perimeter of the square are stalls of all the Rasteau vignerons who fill one's glass, on request, with any of their wines be they red, white or *vin doux*. Looking round the square, one reaches the conclusion that if one takes a glass of each wine offered by all the vignerons, it wouldn't be long before one fell over! One must therefore be selective in the wine on offer, if one is to enjoy all the festivities of the night. Half way round the square we found our favourite Rasteau, the 'Domaine de Papillons' of Didier Charavin.

We were fascinated with the name, which with our favourite brand of Roquefort 'Papillons', and our plate of hand-painted butterflies from the Parisian painter in St. Guilhem-le-Désert make a perfect trio.

More recently Didier changed the name to 'Domaine des Parpaïouns', the *provençal* for butterflies, but this had to be changed (bureaucratic intervention?) to its present name 'Domaine Didier Charavin.' I suspect Didier had similar problems to the Coopérative in Buzet with their top brand, 'Cuvée Napoleon.'

Over the years, we have bought Charavin wines of several vintages, and have never been disappointed. More recently a 'Cuvée Prestige' has been added to the range, and is a regular medal winner at the Concours Général wine fair in Paris. These wines are good examples of inexpensive wines for wine lovers. Like the Juliénas of the Aujas family in the Beaujolais the future of this wine is assured, as father hands over to son, who continues to strive for excellence in each vintage.

Back to the *'Nuit du Vin,'* the village square was well-filled by 9 p.m., when a troop of horsemen (probably from the Camargue) arrived and demonstrated their cowboy skills in the roped enclosure, to the enjoyment of the crowds. The night was a real family affair and at times the children, especially round the food and sweet stalls, seemed to outnumber the adults. Our children were fascinated by a bare-chested, muscular man wearing black leathers and a black leather scull-cap, surrounded by steam, hot oil fumes, the occasional blast of flames from a gas bottle, and an ever present sweet smell of doughnuts. He was operating a machine, which at first glance resembled a steam engine. Into a stainless tub, he added sugar, flour, oil and hot water, and with a big wooden paddle, proceeded to mix a choux pastry. He then filled a simple extruder, and piped a fluted rope of pastry into hot oil, cutting the rope into 3 inch pieces as he oscillated the extruder. After 2 to 3 minutes, he removed the fried pastry and tossed the 'fries' to his female assistant who doused them with sugar and bagged them in tens, for distribution to a never-ending line of eager, salivating customers. Our children naturally joined the queue whilst we ordered pizzas from the pizza van. Anne found a space on one of the trestle tables, I bought a bottle of wine from Didier and fruit drinks for the children, and we all sat back, swaying to the beat and music of the dance band, and enjoyed a simple, very tasty meal, surrounded by throngs of happy revellers. A good night, and definitely worth repeating was the general concensus!

The following day we returned to the village square. It was back to normal, so quiet and still, there was no sign of the previous nights party, had we witnessed 'Brigadoon', I wondered.

On our third Rasteau *'Nuit du Vin,'* the night to celebrate the 30th anniversary of the granting of the Côtes du Rhône Villages status, we were surprised to find that most of the twenty or so Rasteau vignerons who normally offered their wines, were not present and for the night had been replaced by representative teams of vignerons from all the 16 Côtes du Rhône Villages. That night over 10,000 people attended, and what a night!

To taste and compare 16 Côtes du Rhône Villages was an opportunity that could not be missed, and you can rest assured it was not missed! Surprise, surprise, Didier, with son and daughter-in-law, were one of three representative vignerons on the Rasteau stand. All the wines are special, and it is unfair to pick out one particular village, but do buy the wines of Cairanne, Sablet, Vinsobres, Séguret, and St Pantaléon-les-Vignes whilst in the area, and you will not be disappointed.

An additional feature to the night was the presence of street bands playing samba, gypsy and jazz music, modern day Pied Pipers with their band of followers, stopping to pay tribute to each Village wine, as they wandered through the alleys and narrow lanes of Rasteau. The pizza van from our previous nights of wine was also there, and incidentally it is also present, at Vaison-la-Romaine, on market days. Still the husband and wife team, still the delicious *'La Reine'* pizzas. The dance band playing on the stage was now accompanied by laser displays. We could do without the lasers, but not without the pizzas!

Rasteau is just one of many wine villages in this lovely part of France. We would recommend that the wine lover tarry awhile and drink in the atmosphere, the colours, the spectacular countryside, the people, and for a brief period, go native.

The largest town is Vaison-la-Romaine, and as its name suggests dates back to Roman times. It has a Roman museum and part of the town has been carefully excavated to uncover parts of the Roman town with a roman road and villas, and to the amusement of the children, communal toilets. Even more fascinating is the former cathedral of Notre Dame de Nazareth, built almost 900 years ago using parts of Roman pillars as its foundations! Across the River Ouvéze lies the old town of Vaison from whose ramparts can be seen the peak of Mont Ventoux, topped with its statues!

Cross back over the Roman bridge and look out to the hills and try to imagine the happenings of the 22 September 1992, when the gentle river 60 feet below, backed by flash flooding in the mountains cascaded over the bridge, knocked down the parapet, washed away houses and buildings, the bridge at Roaix, caravans, and campers, and claimed the lives of over 40 people, mainly holidaymakers. The power of nature is truly awesome. The flood damage has been repaired, the debris cleared away, a new parapet has been built, there is a new bridge at Roaix, but the watermarks, on the buildings by the Roman bridge in Vaison, still remain as a reminder of the force of nature.

On a happier note, the large colourful market in Vaison-la-Romaine, held every Tuesday, should not be missed. The centre becomes pedestrian-only and is taken over by hundreds of market traders, selling almost everything imaginable. Walking through the market one becomes intoxicated with the variety of aromas, the herbs, spices, garlic, olives, the ripeness and freshness of fruit and vegetables, the smell of the sea in the fish and shellfish, the cheese, newly baked bread, sausage, ham, meat, printed provençal fabrics, leather, and the mouth-watering aromas of cooking paella, pizzas, roasting chickens, and rabbits. All of this, and throngs of locals, catching up on the weekly news, interspersed with jolly holiday visitors, street musicians and occasionally a wandering band of minstrels giving an impromptu concert. Definitely not to be missed.

If you are staying in the area, a ripe melon, with Rasteau, *vin doux* of course, *gambas* in garlic butter, a *baguette*, or even a plate of paella or a pizza from the travelling pizza van, with a bottle of Côtes du Rhône rosé or white, sitting in the shade of a plane tree, makes the ideal lunch.

On our first visit to Vaison-la-Romaine we ate out one night in the Pizzeria in the old town overlooking the river and Roman Vaison, where the owner, having established that we were English, proceeded to tell us in his Provençal-Italian that he loved England and 'Marks and Spencer' and always bought his shirts from there. We have not seen the old man on recent visits, I would like to think he has retired to a rural retreat in southern Italy, leaving the pizzeria in the capable hands of the next generation. With a 'Debussy' and a 'Mozart' pizza it was fitting that we drank Gigondas from the vigneron, Amadieu, (or was it Amadeus) who believe it or not, uses an old disused railway tunnel as a wine cellar!

We eventually found the railway tunnel, outside the village of Pierrelongue, which should also be visited to see the pretty chapel perched on top of a rocky outcrop. On the way back to our gîte, we stopped for a meal in Mollans-s-Ouvéze and part way through our meal we suddenly saw the chef dash out into the garden for some berries, which eventually appeared as decorations on our desert. These berries were the size of grapes, white with red tipped pimples and were very tasty. We subsequently found these berries in a newly created herb garden in Opède-le-Vieux, in the Luberon, and we think we have since identified the fruit as coming from a strawberry tree. We now have such a tree in our garden at home, but to date, it has not fruited, we can only hope.

Whilst driving round the villages seeking out wines, please take time to absorb the beauty of the countryside. We have four favourite views. The view across the valley of the Ouvéze towards Faucon and Puyméras from the road between Mollans and, yet another château-topped village, Entrechaux. The view towards Villedieu and Nyons from the Vaison to Buisson road. The evening view of Cairanne from the high road from St. Romain-de-Malegarde. Finally, my favourite, sunset over Sablet.

There are many picturesque villages, Séguret, well worth a visit to the *salon de thé* for a *thé au citron*, Crestet, Le Barroux, Faucon, and Mollans, all with their narrow cobbled streets, roman wash-houses, fountains and wrought iron belfries. To see nature at its best, a drive through the Dentelles de Montmirial past the sheer-sided village La Roque Alric, takes some beating. If the reader takes time to explore the region, it will be apparent why the Vaucluse has such appeal to the Browns.

Being a lover of wine it is not surprising that I have a passion for grapes, in particular muscat grapes, which when organically grown, freshly picked and eaten unwashed, are out of this world. On one occasion, Madame, the owner of the gîte, brought a basket of muscat grapes from her garden near Mazan and a bottle of white Côtes du Rhône, produced from the vineyards surrounding the gîte, as welcome presents.

Relaxing on the terrace, in the warmth of the early evening, after unpacking the car, surrounded by chirping crickets, in good company, with a glass of cool fresh wine and Muscat grapes, is a glorious way to start a holiday in the Vaucluse. Later that week, driving through the country lanes, we came upon a sign, 'Organically grown muscat grapes for sale.' We stopped at the house, met Monsieur who said the grapes were at his brother's farm across the road and he insisted that he drive us there. Up the bumpy lane in the open topped 2CV to the farmyard and into the barn filled with *plateaux* of grapes. I only wanted a kilogram, but hadn't the heart to purchase anything less than a *plateau*. In spite of eating 10 kilos in less than a week, I still maintain a passion for muscat grapes, but I don't disclose it to the family anymore as it prompts the question "Fancy some grapes Dad?" whereupon the family titters begin, again!

The village of Tulette, is the home of Le Cellier de Dauphins, where prodigious quantities of Côtes du Rhône wines are produced and bottled for the French and UK supermarket trade. It also has a *Pharmacie* for which we shall be ever grateful. After eating *moules*, prepared by Father, Mother became extremely ill and on seeking advice from the *Pharmacienne*, was advised to take natural yoghurt. Within hours the yoghurt cured the sickness.

We have discussed the miraculous properties of yoghurt with friends and have been advised that it is also a very effective cure for sunburn when applied to the affected areas. I suppose this is one further instance of the treatment of ailments without recourse to drugs and medicine. The medical profession is beginning to recognise the value of natural products, after all red wine is now known to assist in reducing Cholesterol levels which adds credibility to the French belief that red wine is good for one!

**Village fountain - Mollans-s-Ouvéze.**

On one of our walks in the region, from Faucon, with its impressive view of Mont Ventoux, to Puyméras, with its three-bell belfry which dominates the village, we found the Coopérative 'Cave La Comtadine'. This is one of the better Coopératives and not only produces a good Côtes du Rhône Villages red but a very good Côtes du Rhône white which is dry, fruity and also has an appealing freshness which is lacking in the more expensive whites from Châteauneuf-du-Pape. This elegant wine is a subtle mixture of Grenache Blanc, Clairette and Ugni Blanc grapes. It is best drunk within one or two years, it is a quality wine and at 25 francs, exceedingly good value. It is one of our favourite wines to drink in the garden on a warm Summer's evening. Almost next door to the Coopérative is the 'Domaine Sainte Apollinaire', where M. et Mme. Daumas produce a range of quality organic reds, predominantly from the Grenache and Syrah grapes.

In this beautiful area with its Roman history, it is fitting that the final paragraphs are devoted to Orange, which not only has a fine Roman Arch de Triomphe but a semi-circular Roman theatre with a 37 metre high southern facade in which classical concerts and operas are held in the Summer months. Our first visit to the theatre was to a centenary Tchaikovsky concert which ended with the 1812 Overture, ably supported by French cannons and fireworks. The Russian orchestra was brilliant but in the final burst of fireworks, during which the whole southern facade was a riot of fire, smoke, and sparks, the whole orchestra had to hurriedly vacate the stage to avoid the debris and cascading sparks. The sight of three double base players in dress suits scurrying across the stage, like a line of penguins each carrying an enormous fish, is forever etched in my memory! On that night we reckoned that the French were the eventual winners!

In the theatre, that night, we happened to sit next to an English couple who were staying 20 miles away near Carpentras, which incidentally also has a very good weekly market, where we were once entertained by the New Orleans buskers playing jazz standards such as 'Sweet Sue' whilst we drank iced Ricard, or have I mentioned that before? The meeting was remarkable in that this couple, who lived near St Albans, had friends in our village, in Yorkshire, whom they had recently visited, and whilst in their garden had admired our house and garden which share a common boundary. I suppose this just goes to show what a small world we live in.

Last year, at the tourist information office in Vaison-la-Romaine, we noticed that Puccini's 'Turandot' was being performed at Orange in the Roman theatre. As the performance was that night, we dashed to Orange to book our seats. All we were offered were seats at 90 francs and 350 francs, and apart from being 3 rows nearer the stage and in a marginally more central position, the extra expense of the 350 francs seats could not be justified. As we had witnessed on our earlier visit, just before the performance was due to begin, the ushers took down their seat signs, and people moved to better seats. This time, being regular theatre-goers, we picked up our cushions and joined the gentle stampede to the higher priced seats. Would you believe, we ended up in the 350 franc seats, nearer the stage and in a more central position than we had been offered in the booking office! A case of when in Rome, or should I say Orange!..... Having saved over £50, we sat back and enjoyed a beautiful night at the Opera and a most memorable 'Nessun Dorma' which was rapturously received by all.

The following Sunday, with the money saved on the Opera, we treated ourselves to Sunday lunch at one of our favourite restaurants the 'St. Hubert' in Entrechaux. All visitors to France must experience Sunday lunch, on a shady terrace of course. At the 'St. Hubert', to enjoy the gastronomic delights, prepared with such loving care by the Mouret family, in the company of enthusiastic happy eaters, is an occasion not to be missed.

There are many other places to visit and treasures to discover in this region, Avignon and its Papal palace, L'Isle-sur-la-Sorgue with its antique street markets and canals, Fontaine-de-Vaucluse, where the crystal clear waters of the River Sorgue emerge from the mountain, the impressive hilltop village of Gordes, Roussillon with its earth pigmented houses and coloured quarries, the tranquillity of the lavender garden at the picturesque Abbaye de Senanque, and many more.

I trust in this chapter that I have whetted the appetite of the reader to visit the region, to enjoy the people, to marvel at the natural beauty and of course, to buy and drink the wine.

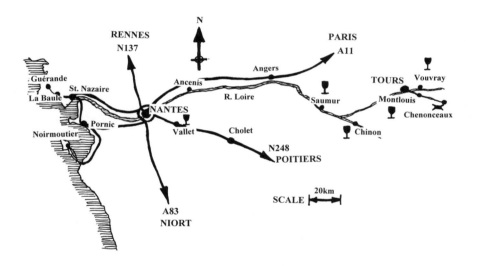

# 9

# Sea salt and Pernod.

This region, the Western Loire, where the Loire, the longest river in France, flows through the city of Tours, the ancient capital of Lorraine, through Saumur and Nantes, past the port and shipbuilding centre of St. Nazaire, into the Atlantic Ocean, is often passed through by British visitors on their way to the south-west and the Dordogne. I must confess the Browns also fall into this category. Perhaps being from the north of England we prefer a more rugged landscape and a little more sun on our backs!

Our first stay, on route to the Medoc, was in a small village outside the city of Tours. This was one of the rare occasions that wine was not the prime objective of the visit, although we did manage to sample a selection of Vouvray wines. Our main objective was to visit the Château de Chenonceau, an architectural gem, which straddles the river Cher, one of the major tributaries of the Loire. This château, built in the 16<sup>th</sup> century and inhabited by Henry II's mistress, and later, by his widow, Catherine de Medici, is probably one of the most attractive of the many châteaux of the Loire. The children imagined that Sleeping Beauty had been imprisoned in one of the many towers. In their imagination, the children could have been near the truth, after all, several formidable ladies had resided there in the past, who might have been tempted to imprison pretty rivals. Looking dreamily at the intricate designs of the formal box-hedged gardens, I swear I felt, for a moment, the presence of courtiers on their post-dinner stroll, discussing matters of the day. I was brought back to reality by excited children imploring me to come and look at the fish in the river.

Over a picnic lunch, not I regret to say of barbecued freshly caught trout, I checked the map and noticed that Chenonceau is also close to the Montlouis and Vouvray vineyards.

A short detour was made to Vouvray, as time did not permit to visit both the vineyards of Montlouis and Vouvray. Both wines are made from the Chenin Blanc grape, but Vouvray has the better reputation as one of the great wines of the Loire. When time permits we will re-visit and carry out a Brown comparative wine tasting! There are many producers of Vouvray but we opted for the respected Coopérative in Vouvray.

Vouvray is the name given to a range of wines, varying from dry to sweet and from still to sparkling. All the wines are produced from the Chenin Blanc grape, which imparts a flowery fruitiness to the wine. The wines can be dry and acidic, especially in years of a poor harvest or sweet when the grapes are late picked, often as late as November. Sparkling Vouvray is made by the *méthode champenoise*. Depending on the individual's preference there is a wine to suit almost any palette, from the dry acidic *'sec'*, through medium-dry *'demi-sec'* and medium-sweet *'demi-doux'* to the luscious sweet *'moelleux.'* The best of the sweetest wine is long lived, made from grapes left on the vine to develop 'noble rot,' and as a consequence is in limited supply and expensive. A comparison of wines made from grapes with 'noble rot' now appears on the Brown's wine tasting wish-list. As if to compensate, in years when a poorly ripened harvest is expected, the vignerons of the region produce semi-sparkling or sparkling Vouvray, which many claim, when at its best, is second only to its north-eastern big brother, Champagne. However I believe the 'sparkler' producers of Saumur and indeed other regions of France would dispute this. Our experience is that, these 'sparkling' Vouvrays are refreshing and pleasant, but lack the intense subtle flavour of real Champagne. Putting it another way, these are everyday wines whereas Champagne is for special occasions.

At the Coopérative we tasted the range of Vouvray but could not agree on which wine to buy, half the team favoured the *'demi-sec'* and half the *'demi-doux,'* so surprise, surprise, we settled on a selection of each. On several comparative tastings at home, opinion is still divided, which only goes to add weight to my earlier point, that Vouvray offers a wine to suit almost any palette. Reluctantly, we rejected the *'sec'* Vouvray because our dry wine allocation for the trip was pre-booked for Muscadet Sevre-et-Maine sur Lie, and the regal Sauvignon Blanc of Sancerre and Pouilly-sur-Loire. We did enjoy the flowery fruity sweetness of the *'moelleux'* and vowed to keep several bottles for 10 years. To the Browns, and the majority of wine drinkers, this is no mean feat. However, if our experiences with long aged Gerwürztraminer are anything to go by, the ageing *'moelleux'* will be well worth waiting for!

That night, a Saturday, we ate, eventually, in an Auberge restaurant. I say eventually because of the inordinate time we had to wait between courses. The food was excellent, but by the time coffee was served I swear we had had three separate meals! Was this an attempt for the 'Guinness Book of Records' or simply a *'manifestation'* by the waiter against 'fast food.' The restaurant was crowded, but there was only one waiter, who was probably doubling up as chef and dishwasher. As the evening wore on, and the pace of the waiter and the frequency of creaks from the ancient oak floorboards slowed, we did finally receive our coffee. Perhaps if we had stood up en masse and given him a round of applause he would have increased his pace on what must have been one of his last laps. I intended to give the waiter a tip, but 'get more staff' was not thought to be in the best interests of *'entente cordiale'* by the family. We returned to our accommodation early in the morning and slept soundly till dawn. Recalling the previous evening, we laughed our way through breakfast.

Suitably refreshed we bade Madame *'au revoir'* and set off for Saumur. Both Anne and I detected the hint of a curious smile on

Madame's face. Perhaps she was recalling the laughter over breakfast of other English visitors who had had similar experiences at the Auberge!

Bypassing Chinon (made a note to visit on a future occasion) we approached Saumur and were immediately struck by the enormity of the Château, which dominates the southern bank of the Loire. However, the best view of the Château is from the north bank of the river, or according to our family of amateur photographers, from the bridge halfway across the Loire. On the street leading up to the Château is the Cave des Vignerons de Saumur, where one can taste not only the basic Saumur Blanc, again made from the Chenin Blanc grape but the *demi-sec* and *brut* sparkling Saumur and the *brut* Crémant de Loire. There is no doubt that the 'sparklers' were more appreciated than the still Saumur and were, in our opinion, equal to, if not superior to, the 'sparkling' Vouvrays of the previous day's tasting. The strong presence of well known Champagne Houses in this area adds substance to this claim. Being significantly lower in price than Champagne, it is easy to see why Saumur *brut* is one of Britain's favourite 'sparklers'. On the whole they are less complex in flavour than Champagne, but I am sure I have detected Chardonnay in addition to Chenin Blanc in some of the higher quality Saumur. There is also an interesting Crémant de Loire rosé which is made from the Cabernet Franc grape and would make an interesting comparison with Crémant de Bourgogne rosé. However, the Cabernet Franc is truly at its best in the Saumur Champigny, where the heady raspberry aroma with a slight earthy flavour matures into smooth richness on ageing. We particularly like this rich, but uncomplicated wine, and enjoy it with food with delicate flavours, where a more robust gutsy wine, such as a Côtes du Rhône would dominate, to the detriment of the food.

Although these Loire wines are enjoyable, they do not appeal to the Browns as much as those of the Rhône, Burgundy or Bordeaux.

**Saumur.**

I think the difference is one of association, it is not just the quality of the wine that gives pleasure, nor the fact that one has found one of good value, but more the memory of the taste; the hot balmy day, the warmth of the sun, the enthusiastic vigneron, the countryside, the complexity of flavours. It is only when all these aspects are brought together that wine drinking is truly enjoyable.

Having said all that, there are always exceptions to the rule, and for me it is the lure of the sea. Being a 'sand grown un' from Lancashire, I have always had an affection for the coast and the sea.

The salty air, the ozone, the shrieking of the gulls, the whirling swarms of dunlins over the mud flats, the low flying packs of oyster catchers, the noise of the sea from becalmed ripples to crashing breakers, remind me of happy Summer days as a child, and the smells, sights and sounds will always be with me. We left Saumur for the coast of South Brittany, and, as we passed through Nantes, I swear I could smell the sea!

We stayed in Pornic, a charming small fishing port and unspoilt seaside resort, which looks as though it has changed little since the turn of the century when it was 'discovered by well-heeled French town dwellers'. The coast walks, north and south of Pornic are beautiful, and bracing, and even on breezy days, one can find sheltered, sandy coves, to enjoy an invigorating swim in the fresh, pure, clear waters of the Atlantic. The breakers, on windy days, crash over the rocks creating great plumes of spray, after all the nearest land to the west is America! Totally refreshed by a swim, what could be better than a plate of fresh oysters, with a twist of lemon, washed down with a glass or two of Muscadet de Sèvre-et-Maine sur Lie, or the crispy dry Gros Plant sur Lie. Not a lot! There are people who say that one should drink Champagne with oysters, but the Browns always believe that the locals know best, and in this area where there is a strong dependence on the fruits of the sea, it is not surprising that the complimentary crisp dry wines are also produced here.

Of the wines of the Western Loire, these two wines are highly placed in the Brown's premier list of good drinking wines. Every time we have sea food or oysters with Muscadet or Gros Plant at home, the association with Pornic, the walks on the seashores of the idyllic Ile de Noirmoutier, and the sensual memories, all add to the enjoyment of the meal.

But where to taste and buy the wine? As we have said before, wine purchased from the producer always tastes better than that purchased from the supermarket. Our recommendation is therefore, to visit the Coopérative in Vallet, in the centre of the Muscadet Sèvre-et-Maine vineyards. There are 36 vignerons in this Coopérative, and all bottle their own wine, and each grower's wine is on sale. By all means taste two or three, but do not attempt all 36! Needless to say all the wines are good, and by keeping the wine in the barrel with the sediment until the time of bottling *(sur lie)* the vignerons add a distinctive and agreeable flavour to the wine. Gros Plant sur Lie is also available, and although slightly drier and crisper than Muscadet Sèvre-et-Maine sur Lie, is still a good wine. They also sell simple Muscadet for a few francs less, but the quality of the wine is significantly less than the *sur lie* wines. Stuck with the question of which vigneron's wine to buy, the Browns usually buy two or three mixed cases, with the intention of selecting at home, a preferred vigneron for the next purchasing trip. However, we never agree, so not surprisingly, we end up buying mixed cases on the next visit! I think over the years we have tried all 36 vignerons' wines and have never been disappointed, which in itself is a recommendation of the quality of wine from this Coopérative. There are two additional advantages to the wine drinker, these wines are inexpensive, and do not occupy cellar space for long, as they should be drunk within two to three years!

Whilst in the area one must visit the Ile de Noirmoutier, but only cross via the Passage du Gois when the tide is out, otherwise you may have to spend hours marooned in the refuge tower! Noirmoutier is a bustling town which amongst the tourist trappings also sells a culinary gem, Noirmoutier sea salt. This salt has a superb flavour, and is 'farmed' from the sea using the salt pan technique. However, unlike the piles of salt from the Camargue which have a pink colour, this salt is sandy coloured. There are many miles of sandy coastline scattered with whitewashed, blue shuttered fishermen's cottages. What a beautiful place to drop out and become a beachcomber! One day, maybe!

Standing one morning at a harbour wall, on the peninsular, we were fascinated by the antics of a rotund French grandpa and his small grandson. They were catching small silvery fish, similar to whitebait, for their evening meal, using a small scale version of the square nets used on the rocky coastline of Brittany. The net, approximately one metre square, had a weight attached to its centre and was raised and lowered using a rope and pulley on a jib.

The grandpa was obviously the brains of the team and the young lad was his labourer. The grandson lowered the net into the water, grandfather then dropped a small ball of flour/bran paste into the net and within seconds, numerous hungry, small fish attacked the paste ball. On a signal from grandpa, the grandson hauled up the net, the grandfather dropped the fish into a bucket, and the whole operation was repeated. It wasn't long before the bucket was full of fish! An inquisitive Dutch couple questioned the old man on why the fish when he dropped them into the bucket, appeared to die. The old man looking into the bucket of now cloudy water, and said it was the Pernod in the water which had made the fish drunk. I must admit the water did have the same cloudy appearance as when Pernod is added to water, but the Dutch couple actually believed him! After they had left the old man turned to us, shrugged his shoulders and muttered "Pernod, do they think I am mad!" It transpired that the old man was camping with the extended family, and his contribution was to catch the supper, whilst at the same time passing on his skills to his eager young grandson. I envied that man. Perhaps one day I will be in the fortunate position of handing down some of my skills to my grandson.

Later that afternoon, on the harbour side, we ordered a Pernod rather than our usual Ricard, and come to think of it, when the iced water was added it did resemble the contents of the old man's bucket!

Reluctantly we left the island and because the tide was in, had to return over the toll bridge but the toll booths had been removed some time previously; the power of the people on the Government no doubt. Later during our stay we crossed the Loire, over the St Nazaire bridge which offers superb views of the St. Nazaire shipyards from its elevated carriageway. Again no tolls, yet on our earlier visit the toll was 40 francs, another success for people power! Perhaps the British people should adopt French attitudes to the Severn, Forth and Humber bridges! Continuing past St. Nazaire to the fashionable resort of La Baule and then on across the salt pans one reaches Guérande, an interesting old walled town with four medieval gateways and many old houses and alleyways. A pleasant place to brouse.

All the Browns enjoy shellfish, but can I persuade any of them to eat snails, no way! During our last visit to the area, I picked up a leaflet for guided visits to an *escargot* farm at St. Etienne de Mer Morte. I gently broached the possibility of a visit, but was given a veiled threat that, if I insisted, there was every possibility that the *'mer morte'* would live up to its name. I do now have one convert, our daughter Cheryl is now married, and our *beau-fils*, John, to his credit, and my delight, is an *escargot* fan. Perhaps we will visit the farm, one day!

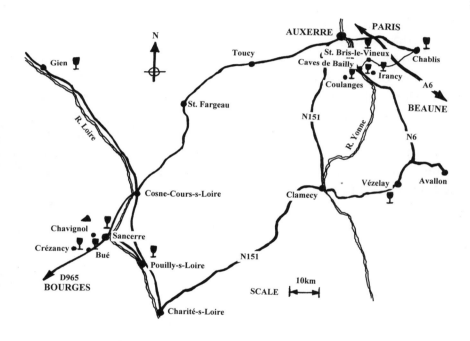

# 10

# Auntie Frances and Pouilly Fumé.

$T$he River Loire, at approximately 1000km., the longest river in France, from its source on the mountain 'Gerbier de Jonc' in the Cevennes, flows north, then north-west, and finally west, to St Nazaire on the Atlantic coast.

Almost halfway upstream from St Nazaire lies the hilltop town of Sancerre, arguably the home of the best wines made from the Sauvignon Blanc grape. Other countries, especially New Zealand, would argue this point, and claim that their style of Sauvignon Blanc wines are better. The Brown opinion is, that although the New Zealand wines are crisp dry and fruity, they are different to Sancerre. With the strong citrus flavours, especially lemons and grapefruit, the wine growers in New Zealand have created a very appealing, high quality wine, but of a different style to traditional Sauvignon Blanc wines such as Sancerre. My own opinion, which is not necessarily that of the Brown family tasting panel, is that South American Sauvignon Blanc wines have the potential to become serious competitors to the traditional Sauvignon Blanc wines. Until that time we will continue to buy and enjoy the excellent wines of Sancerre and its less well known but equally appealing neighbour Pouilly-sur-Loire. After all, how would we manage to bring back a car boot of wine from South America?

Being located in the centre of France the wine drinker has to decide on which way to approach Sancerre. From the west, having tasted and purchased wines of the Western Loire, drive along the Loire valley to Blois with its historic castle, taking a short detour, if on the château run, to Chambord. Continue, via Orleans with its impressive statue to Joan of Arc, taking, if time permits, a detour to

Bourges to marvel at the splendour of the gothic Cathedral, to Sully-sur-Loire, with its fairy tale style moated, turreted castle. Onward through Gien, with its famous Museum of Hunting, located in the castle, to Cosne-sur-Loire, crossing the Loire and its adjacent canal, to the hilltop town of Sancerre.

An alternative route, having purchased wine from Bordeaux region would be to drive north-east via Limoges, resisting if possible the female cries to stop and admire (nay buy) delicate Limoges porcelain, through Bourges, to approach Sancerre from its most photogenic side. On one occasion we stopped to admire the view of Sancerre, the town squatting comfortably atop of rolling vine-clad hillsides. What a view! Across the road was the local football ground, it must be the best located ground anywhere, with a view like that I would have played my socks off!

As I am constantly reminded, there is only one alternative, so another option, en route from the Chablis region would be to drive through Auxerre, to St. Bris-le-Vineux, purchasing the easy drinking Sauvignon St. Bris, (purely for comparative tasting purposes back home). Then to drive along the banks of the River Yonne, via Avallon (don't forget to play the tape Dad!) and the hilltop village of Vézelay, with its impressive abbey-church of La Madeleine, to the Loire, at La Charité-sur-Loire, and finally northwards to Sancerre.

Yet another option, for visitors from the Burgundy region, would be to travel through the Morvan National Park, via Autun and Château Chinon (don't forget to visit the museum) to cross the Loire, at Pouilly-sur-Loire, and approach Sancerre through its southern vineyards.

For longer distance travellers, returning from the Rhône and the Languedoc Roussillon areas, with a heavy load, enjoy an extremely pleasant motorway drive via St. Etienne, along the A72, with superb views of the unspoilt French countryside (in marked contrast to the overcrowded M5/M6 motorways around

Birmingham) and, at Clermont-Ferrand, turn north onto the A71 to Bourges, and across country, to Sancerre.

Having decided on the route to Sancerre, driven around and up the hill to the central square, the wine drinker is now ready to seek out the nectar of Sancerre. A word of caution, the central square, the Nouvelle Place, has several strategically placed *ralentiers* (sleeping policemen) which can cause embarrassing scraping noises if one's vehicle is heavily laden as we have experienced on a couple of occasions! The staff, in the *Office de Tourisme*, are extremely helpful, and will point the weary traveller in the right direction for good food, accommodation and of course, good wine.

**Sancerre and its vineyards.**

Our favourite Sancerre is produced by the Vacheron family, and although it can be purchased from their shop in the Nouvelle Place it somehow tastes better when bought direct from the cave.

On our first visit to Sancerre several years ago, we were walking around the village, as lost tourists do, when we were approached by an elderly Frenchman, who having established that we were English and not German, became very chatty. He went on to explain his initial coolness. During the last war, he and the many young men of Sancerre were forced to spend many nights away from home in the woods and vineyards, for fear of the Germans and he had never really forgiven them for this. As to the vote on the Maastricht Treaty he would definitely vote *"Non."* We were not surprised when the French people finally voted, but only by a very narrow majority, to accept the Treaty.

The old man's face brightened, and, with a twinkle in his eye, he started to enthuse about the jewel of Sancerre, its wine! As if the Browns needed any convincing! But where to taste? He produced a street map, in English, of course, and pointed out the location of several vignerons who had cellars under the narrow streets. Salivating at the prospect, we thanked the old man for his kindness and proceeded to seek out the Vacherons.

Was that Auntie Frances standing in the gateway? If it wasn't, then she has a very convincing double, I thought. As we approached, she greeted us, and asked if we would like to visit the Vacheron caves. Would we like to visit, had we not driven halfway across France for this opportunity! But where were the caves? She bade us follow through a door, down well-trodden stairs into a labyrinth of cellars under the house, courtyard and the street. We followed her, past wine making machinery, rows of maturing wine in oak casks, past the bottling plant, into the tasting room. Who would have believed that Aladdin's cave did indeed exist, here in Sancerre! We reverently tasted Sancerre Blanc from two vintages, what a taste, dry, flinty fruitiness with a long lingering aftertaste. We then tasted rosé, a pleasant light Summer aperitif, and rouge, similar to a young lightweight Burgundy, and according to 'Auntie Frances' a very fashionable wine for drinking chilled with fish. Both wines are made from the Pinot Noir grape. At this point I must echo the words of Arthur Eperon who wrote in his 'Eperon's French Wine Tour'[3], on the subject of young red Sancerre, "To me it tastes raw. Pinot Noir does not make wines for drinking very young. Ask them in Beaune."

We purchased two cases of white, one of each vintage, and a few bottles of rouge, which I must say with a couple of years bottle age although very light, proved very enjoyable. While waiting for the Access to be accepted, Anne noticed a bottle of Sancerre with a Fortnum and Mason label. "Yes, we supply the London store" said 'Auntie Frances.' After much haggling we managed to persuade 'Auntie' to part with a bottle. *"Un cadeau pour notre fils,"* said Anne. On our way back to the car, Anne remembered that we had some Fortnum and Mason tea bags in the car, so we packed the wine, and retraced our steps to find 'Auntie.' She was so pleased when we gave her a couple of tea bags as a *petit cadeau!* To this day we always remember 'Auntie,' when we open a bottle of Vacheron Sancerre.

That night, after almost two weeks of excellent French four and five course meals, we ate for a change, in a local pizzeria. It is surprising, after nights of rich food, how appetising basic pizzas, with a simple green salad can be. Over a bottle of Sancerre Rouge we recalled our experiences with French pizzas. We remembered the well-chillied pizza oil in Arras. Used to drizzling Nyons pizza oil we did not heed the warning of the waiter that the oil was *trés fort,* it took three bottles of cold beer to bring the taste buds back to room temperature!

We remembered the excellent hand-made pizzas in Mâcon, washed down with pitchers of Beaujolais, made memorable the following morning, when checking the Access receipt, in the full light of day, we found the amount had been incorrectly entered, the decimal point was in the wrong place and we had only been charged 10% of the bill, or perhaps that night there was a 90% discount!

"The 'Debussy' in Vaison takes some beating" said Anne. In the end we agreed that pizzas from the van at the Rasteau night of wine were the best, and vowed to re-affirm our conclusions on our next visit to the Vaucluse.

The following morning, after fresh croissants and coffee, we visited the village of Bué, to buy Sancerre from a local vigneron, but which one? We finally decided on a vigneron called Rix (in our earlier life we had used heating oil supplied by Rix Petroleum Ltd), if he made as good a wine as his namesake's heating oil, then we would not be disappointed. He might also be funny with it!

It was 10 a.m., not the ideal time to taste sharp dry Sancerre, and not with taste-buds still savouring the residual flavours of croissants and coffee. The sight of two English people with faces like dried prunes, prompted M. Rix to ask if the wine was too cold. This could almost have been a scene from one of the 'Whitehall Farces', perhaps there is a connection with his British name sake after all! We explained the reason for our reaction. He laughed, and by the third glass our palette had adjusted to the astringency of his wine, and we were back in the tasting groove. Rix's wine was drier and definitely sharper than that from Vacheron. We purchased a case and thought it would suit shellfish, especially oysters, as an alternative to Muscadet Sèvre-et-Maine sur'Lie or the sharper Gros Plant sur Lie wines from the Nantais.

Had time permitted, we would have tasted wines of the vignerons in other villages such as Crézancy, Sury-en-Vaux and Chavignol. On subsequent visits we have tasted wines from these villages and found them all to be of a consistently high standard, but, to select one as being better than another has, like the Muscadet wines from Vallet, proved impossible. The village of Chavignol has a more important claim to fame than being a Sancerre producing village, it has given its name to an unusual goats cheese, *'Crottin de Chavignol'*. One should not be put off by its name nor indeed its appearance, and one should, as we did on that Bué day, seek out the

Caves de la Mignonne, which are located to the left of the D955 from Bourges, in the outskirts of Sancerre. Here one can taste the cheese, with its natural wine partner Sancerre, the flavours blend well together. As the locals on the Atlantic coast have found their local Nantais wines to be the ideal, natural accompaniment to shellfish, so it is with *'Crottin de Chavignol'* and Sancerre.

As we have found out many times in France, you can save yourself time and effort in finding good food and wine by talking to, and taking advice from, the locals.

The following morning while enjoying a coffee on the ramparts, we witnessed the whistle-stop coach tour of Sancerre. We heard the coach straining up the hill long before we could see it, and eventually it came around the corner and with a grateful hiss of air-brakes halted outside one of the tasting shops on the main road. With another hiss, the door opened and a gaggle of tourists decanted onto the pavement and were shepherded into the tasting rooms. Within 10 minutes they returned, slightly merrier, clutching their three packs, and filed in orderly fashion back onto the coach. Whilst this was happening the driver was loading a couple of cases into the luggage hold, obviously his commission! Within a minute the coach door closed, the engine was started and the coach departed, next stop Beaune?

Nothing was said, it wasn't necessary, we knew the best way to tour the wine regions of France, I bet the coach passengers never meet their 'Auntie Frances'.

Earlier in this chapter, I made reference to the neighbouring village of Pouilly-sur-Loire, and its excellent wines. Two wines are produced, a quaffable, youthful, easy drinking Pouilly-sur-Loire and a powerful serious wine, Pouilly Fumé. The former is made from the Chasselas grape and the latter from the Sauvignon Blanc grape. Although the grapes are grown on the east bank of the River Loire, opposite Sancerre, the *terroir* and the vignerons' skills produce, in their Pouilly Fumé, wines which are significantly different to

Sancerre. These wines tend to be less fruity than Sancerre but with a flinty slightly smokier flavour, and a continuing after taste. The wine lover, if possible, should seek out vignerons who also produce Pouilly Fumé from selected old vines, as these wines are superb having a mellow fruitiness which is enhanced by the smokiness.

There is one place to stop in Pouilly-sur-Loire, the Caves de Pouilly-sur-Loire, 'Les Moulins à Vent', the Coopérative where the grapes of seven communes are lovingly converted into beautiful wine. The added bonus being, that literally, across the road, is the 'Relais Fleuri' and its excellent restaurant 'Le Coq Hardi.' To the lover of wine, food, and French ambience, this place takes some beating! The hotel gardens slope gently down to the River Loire and a pre-dinner glass, or two, of chilled fruity Pouilly-sur-Loire, in the garden, at the end of a tiring day should not be missed. A gastronomic dinner, lovingly prepared by the proprietor/chef, with a bottle of Pouilly Fumé Vieilles Vignes from the Coopérative, and a glass of Armagnac over coffee brings a perfect day to a close.

One morning, a short leisurely, after breakfast walk, along the banks of the Loire, marvelling at the width of the river almost 500 kilometres from the sea, watching a couple of herons, watching their breakfast, was interrupted by a rapidly approaching car. The car screeched to a halt, and an agitated Frenchman, surrounded by a car full of fractious kids, and I guess, approx.50% of the contents of his house, (the remaining 50% being precariously stacked on the roof), obviously on his annual pilgrimage to the Med. asked if this was the way to the N7! His wife, who I swear was looking at the map upside-down, had obviously sent the distraught fellow down the wrong road. I resisted the temptation to ask if this narrow road, little wider than a cart track, really looked like a *Route Nationale*, and politely suggested that he should turn left at the bridge, then right, and after 2 kilometres, the road would join the N7. He thanked us profusely, bad-mouthed his wife, and sped off. We fell about laughing, we had at last met a real French family going on their annual holidays! On subsequent occasions when we find ourselves lost, rather than blame the navigator, all that is necessary, to break the tension, is the word N7!

Remembering our experiences on early morning tastings after coffee, we decided to delay our tasting until the afternoon. We paid a visit to La Charité-sur-Loire, an ancient town, which from the remaining parts of its 11th century walls and castle offers good views of the old town and the river Loire. Apparently this was one walled town that Joan of Arc besieged but never captured! After a pleasant walk in the old town, we dined al fresco with bread, Bayonne ham, slivers of Camembert and a delightful bottle of Sancerre Rosé. With taste buds at the ready we returned to Pouilly to visit the Coopérative.

We were surprised to find Coteaux du Giennois rouge and rosé wines, made from Gamay and Pinot Noir grapes, but found them inferior to Beaujolais and Sancerre rosé, so even though they appealed on price, our limited wine space was reserved for the Pouilly wines. First the Pouilly-sur-Loire, light unsophisticated and fruity with no pretentions to being anything other than party wine. Next Pouilly Fumé, the initial dry fruitiness being overlaid with a faint smokiness. It was only this hint of smokiness which distinguished it from Sancerre. Finally to the Pouilly Fumé Vieilles Vignes, what a gem! A rounder, more intensely flavoured wine than the Pouilly Fumé with a fantastic after taste, definitely in a class of its own. It was so good we even asked for a second glass! We had no difficulty in deciding to purchase two cases of Vieilles Vignes and a half case of the ordinary Fumé. Whilst we had been tasting a long table had been laid in the adjoining room, for a party, we were told. I made a note, the venue for a special birthday or wedding anniversary meal, perhaps?

If time, and wine space, permits, a mini tour of the vineyards around the ancient capital of Berry, Bourges, is a good way of buying reasonably priced dry Sauvignon Blanc wines. Of these Menetou-Salon is the best, and resembles a Sancerre with some of the corners knocked off, and is of importance to the wine lover, in being less expensive than Sancerre or Pouilly Fumé.

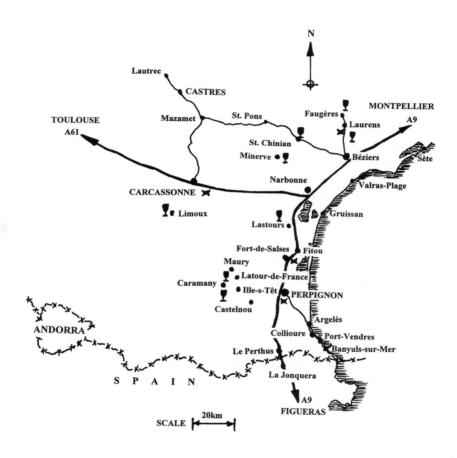

N

MONTPELLIER

TOULOUSE
A61

Lautrec
CASTRES
Mazamet
St. Pons
Faugères
Laurens
A9
St. Chinian
Minerve
Béziers
Sète
Narbonne
CARCASSONNE
Valras-Plage
Limoux
Gruissan
Lastours
Fort-de-Salses
Fitou
Maury
Latour-de-France
Caramany
Ille-s-Têt
PERPIGNON
Castelnou
Argelès
Colioure
Port-Vendres
ANDORRA
Banyuls-sur-Mer
Le Perthus
La Jonquera
SPAIN
A9
FIGUERAS
SCALE
20km

# 11

# After-shave and Garlic.

At the time of our earlier visit to the Midi and Languedoc-Roussillon, after years of avoiding the wines from the 'French wine lake,' with their reputation for being cheap and cheerful, we found that, at last, the vignerons were forsaking quantity for quality. Our attention was again drawn to this area by a remarkable range of wines promoted by 'Bottoms Up', which not only featured the excellent red from Mas de Daumas Gassac, about which I have already enthused at length, but quality wines from Corbières, Faugères, Minervois, St. Chinian, Coteaux du Languedoc and Côtes du Roussillon. To the Browns, who enjoy drinking quality wines at realistic prices, these wines certainly passed the test!

From a vague 'we should re-visit' from our earlier journey to the region, a second visit suddenly became top priority.

We decided to stay in a hotel in Argelès, close to the picturesque, former fishing village of Collioure, which more recently has become a haunt of painters attracted to the area by the intensity of the light, the interesting old town, the imposing castle, and the diminishing fleet of brightly coloured anchovy fishing boats.

On our way to Argelès we made one mistake. We decided, after a long hot drive from the Beaujolais region, to exit the autoroute at Perpignan, this being the shortest route to Argelès. This did not prove to be the shortest route in time, as we hit Perpignan at rush hour, on a Friday! After a hot drive, (we did not have the luxury of air-conditioning) to be within 15 miles of a refreshing cool shower, to be delayed by almost two hours, seemed a trifle unfair, to put it mildly! After all I have said about traffic jams in Britain, give me the M25 please. No, I don't really mean that, nothing could be worse than the M25, unless of course it is the M5/M6, or the M42, or the M1, or the M62 etc.

Eventually we reached the hotel, showered, and with a large iced gin and tonic by the pool, very quickly forgot the *'confiture' de Perpignan!*

**Collioure from the vineyards.**

More recently we travelled south on the Autoroute on a Saturday morning in mid-August and the traffic, heading north from Spain and the French coast, seemed to be bumper-to-bumper all the way from the Spanish border to Narbonne, a distance of 90 kilometres. How we felt for those convoys of Dutch caravan-owners, who obviously started early to beat the traffic. It would take them another week at that rate to get home! I recall earlier holidays in France when the children asked why is it that the Dutch always travel in two's? After some time debating the subject we confessed that we could not find a logical answer. Perhaps Cheryl's comment at the time, of "It's all double Dutch to me!" is still applicable today, but nowadays with the increase in motor traffic needs updating to treble or quadruple!

I digress, back to the main story. The view from our hotel balcony across the foothills to the mountains of the Pyrenees was stunning. With map and binoculars we identified Tour Madeloc, which we visited the following day on our breath-taking drive through the steep-sided vineyards of the Collioure region, but we couldn't see the hotel from the Tour Madeloc!

The wine drinker must drive through the Collioure vineyards to fully appreciate the difficulty the vignerons have in tending the vines and in gathering the grapes. The vineyards are planted on steep hillsides in the most inaccessible places. There are a few hairy parts on the road, especially near the Tour Madeloc, but the views on the drive are magnificent. To the north, the flat expanse of beaches from Argelès-Plage to St. Cyprien-Plage stretching as far as the eye can see, and beyond to Sète and the Camargue. To the west, the vineyards tumbling down to the azure blue Mediterranean Sea, the fishing village resorts of Collioure, Port Vendres, to the south-west, Banyuls and the Spanish border and, finally, to the south and east, the ever present Pyrenees. It is easy to see why, with such a beautiful view, wafted by the warm salty sea breeze, that these grapes produce such a special wine. If I was a vine I couldn't think of a better place to grow up! The twisting road eventually descends to Banyuls-sur-Mer and the tasting rooms of the Celliers des Templiers.

It was late morning when we arrived at the Celliers des Templiers. It was hot and sunny, without a breath of air and the only sound was the crunching of our feet on the pea gravel of the courtyard. It was so still and deserted, almost dream-like, and for a second I was with the 'Magnificent Seven' in a Mexican village half expecting to be ambushed as we searched for signs of life. We eventually found a closed door with a small sign *'Ouvert.'* We gingerly opened it and walked into a dimly lit passage which led into a large room with a bar where two people were engaged in quiet conversation. *"Pardon monsieurs, le caveau, est-il ouvert?"* I asked timidly. *"Oui, monsieur"* replied the smaller man, as he turned to face us.

Clean shaven with hair slicked back, wearing neatly-pressed, dark charcoal trousers, a crisp white shirt and black dickie-bow, and reeking of aftershave, we were taken completely by surprise. Perhaps we had come to the wrong place, was this a seedy nightclub? He then asked if we would like to see a video film and we were ushered into a small room to be followed by a young couple who we had previously noticed lurking outside. This could be different I thought! The video started and the fantasising was over, it was a video on wine after all!

As well as making wine, they also produce a *vin doux*, which is superior to the Grenache *vin doux* from Rasteau and indeed this *vin doux*, Banyuls Grand Cru, is rated as good as vintage port in some quarters. Outside we had noticed rows of old barrels bleaching in the sun, which we were informed contained maturing *vin doux*, where presumably a degree of oxidation takes place to give the 'rancio' flavour.

Our natty host then took us into the cellars where he enthused about the best of the Grand Crus, which improved with age, both in flavour and in price! He also said that the caves were conditioned to assist in bringing the fortified wine to perfection. Funny I thought, does his aftershave affect the maturing process?

Finally the tasting, we started with a Collioure rosé which was absolutely stunning, a balanced mixture of Grenache and Syrah grapes which gave the wine intense but yet elegant, flavours and aromas of luscious, ripe, red fruits. A very good rosé indeed. We decided that one day we should arrange a blind rosé tasting to compare Bergerac rosé, Tavel, Gigondas rosé, Lirac, Collioure rosé with lesser rosés from Provence, Charente and the Midi. We believe that the reputed best rosé, Tavel, would be under intense competition!

The rosé was followed with their Collioure red, Château Reig, a rich dark glorious wine produced from the best grapes grown on the steep terraces by the Mediterranean, and lovingly aged in *barriques*, deep in the Château's caves. The wine is very good and an ideal wine to serve with duck, but is rather expensive, no doubt reflecting the difficulties in growing and harvesting grapes on hillsides. Perhaps the price is the reason why we see so little of this wine in the UK, a great pity, because it really is a special wine. All I know is that when I taste this wine at home, I close my eyes and am transported to the Banyuls hillsides, where I can feel and taste the salt and ozone in the gentle warming breeze from the Mediterranean. You just do not get that 'buzz' from drinking supermarket wines!

The young couple declined to purchase and left. As we were obviously intent on purchasing wine, our perfumed host became more enthusiastic and introduced the Browns to Banyuls Grand Cru, one of the best *vin doux* in France. Unlike other *vin doux*, these fortified wines do indeed taste like port, and vintage Banyuls, carefully aged for 15-20 years and more, is comparable and similar to, quality vintage port. It also, like vintage port, commands high prices! We bought a few bottles of a mid-priced vintage and found to our surprise that whereas we would normally drink these wines with cheese, the best Banyuls, because of its oxidised sweet raisin taste, is also ideal with chocolate and chocolate-based desserts. I must admit I was sceptical at the time, when Mr. 'Aftershave' suggested Banyuls and chocolate, but he was right!

Being close to the Spanish border the Browns decided to continue along the coast road to Spain. After the old French border village of Cerbère, the coastal road becomes more tortuous with an increasing number of tight hairpin bends into Spain. We were disappointed with this part of Spain as the area looked to be in economic decline, probably due to lack of tourism. This may have been one of the main routes into Spain in the past, but the advent of modern transport, and the building of the Autoroute, 25 km. inland, probably hastened the economic decline of this region. Perhaps now we are all Europeans the prosperity enjoyed in Collioure and Banyuls, due in no small part to tourism, may filter into this equally rugged coastline.

We did not have a map with us, so, at Llansa, we decided to follow the road to Figueras and signs pointing to the Autoroute. Within a short time we had left behind the rugged coast and were driving across the plain, when surprise, surprise, it started to rain! This prompted a noisy rendition of 'The rain in Spain falls mainly on the plain'. Boy did it rain! After 15 km. with the only notable feature being a 'San Miguel' brewery/bottling plant we reached Figueras. Driving in a foreign country with a minimal understanding of the language and without a phrase book can be frustrating, but without a map and no Sun to determine direction, it can become impossible! Driving round and round Figueras, in the rain, to find signs for the Autoroute north, to France, became a challenge. After several failed attempts to escape the town, the rain relented briefly and with the Sun at our backs we headed northwards, and after a short while, found the Autoroute. The rain restarted with a vengeance and so we decided to stop at the next town, La Jonquera, for refreshment.

La Jonquera just happens to be last town in Spain on the road to France and has all the trappings of a successful, tacky, border town, hotels, lorry parks, restaurants, bars and inevitably supermarkets. Through the blinding rain, gingerly avoiding the puddles we dived into a café and enjoyed a most welcome large milky coffee. Having no pesetas, we paid for the drinks in francs and were given 50 pesetas in change, but more of this later. As we finished our coffee, the rain slackened, and seizing the opportunity, we dashed across the road into one of the larger supermarkets. While Anne looked for anchovies, I just happened to gravitate to the wine and spirit section. Actually one could hardly miss it as it occupied at least 50% of the store space. The choice, particularly of spirits was staggering, and the prices unbelievable. Ricard at £7 a litre, Gordon's gin at £4.50 a bottle, it was not surprising that most of the shoppers had trolleys full of spirits. I weakened, I decided that I would replace the boot-space reserved for one of the cases of wine with a case of gin, after all we do drink the odd gin and tonic back home, and more to the point, a saving of £60 on a case of gin compared to UK prices was not to be sniffed at! The gin and anchovies helped overcome the disappointment of our wet drive into Spain.

On the French side of the border lies le Perthus, another thriving, but less tacky town which also owes its wealth to the sale of wine and spirits. On other trips to France we have found there to be a similar booming trade in wine and spirits on the Italian border near Ventimiglia!

If we are ever near the two borders the order is 'Gin and anchovies' or 'Gin and parmesan and dried porcini'.

Perhaps when Scotland and Wales become totally independent of England we could have similar wine and spirit supermarkets on the borders! Well, one can only dream.

Seriously, we would like some-one to explain to the Browns, why duty-free spirits purchased at UK airports and on Channel ferries are always more expensive than spirits bought from these border towns and are often no cheaper than spirits bought duty-paid from French supermarkets. It is our opinion that the duty-free suppliers prefer to enjoy higher profit margins rather than pass the savings onto the customer.

On a more humorous note, we rejoined the Autoroute at La Jonquera, and immediately had to pay a toll, 40 pesetas (16p) so our change from the café came in handy. At the next booth a French couple handed over a 100 franc note and received a bag of potatoes (sorry pesetas) as change, we collapsed with mirth, it really made our day! On a subsequent visit we found ourselves without pesetas but were allowed to pay by Access, for 16p, could that happen in the UK, I doubt it!

The reader will recall, in an earlier chapter I mentioned that the Browns had stayed in a hotel in the region and met a Liverpool lass, who had met and spoken with President Clinton, (no, her name was not Monica), whose husband introduced us to a glorious Beaujolais-Villages wine which he bought from his wine maker in a small village to the north-west of Lyon. At dinner in the hotel that night, the food was good but the wine, a Côtes du Roussillon Villages from Caramany, was excellent. It was not surprising therefore, that the following day we should find ourselves driving through the Agly valley to Caramany, one of two Côtes du Roussillon Villages allowed to use the village name on the bottle, the other being, Latour de France. As one approaches the village, the man-made lake on the Agly gives one the impression that Caramany is a lakeside village, but this is an illusion.

Driving through and out of the village on the approach to the 'lake of Agly,' one reaches the Coopérative, where a range of superior Roussillon wines, rich and long in flavour, and very good value, are produced. We particularly liked the oak aged wine which after 5 years is fulfilling its promise and will keep for at least another 10 years. A very good wine indeed!

Pleased with our purchase, we decided that we should drive down the Agly valley and visit the other superior village, Latour de France. It was on the road to Latour de France that I made my biggest gaff. Like many families with children on holiday, the Browns, on long car journeys, held competitions, after 'I spy,' counting 'Norberts', counting 'Eddys,' ticking off the 95 *départements* of French car number-plates, who can make the most disgusting 'raspberry' sound, we now only keep a tally of 'gaffs', usually on a 1-10 scale. A score of 4-5 is normal but to achieve a 10, the 'gaff' has to be memorable. Whilst still savouring the luscious wine from Caramany, driving through the gently undulating countryside, through wall-to-wall vineyards, enjoying the warmth and brightness of the Sun, the fresh smell of the open air, I was brought back to reality by Anne, who was navigating, saying "Latour de France." Where-upon I looked round and, unable to see any cyclists, made the fatal mistake of replying, "Where?" She would not believe that I really meant to say, "Where, I didn't see the road sign." To this day I have been unable to convince anyone that my comment did not warrant a 10! However, I believe that one member of the family, I dare not say which one, made the biggest 'gaff' ever, a good 10+, when standing on the beach at Argelès, pointed left when asked which way to Spain!

Although only 10 km. from Caramany, wines from Latour de France are softer and more immediately drinkable. The vines growing on granite and schist, give the wine backbone and therefore it is not necessary to add tannins from oak ageing to produce longevity. This wine is therefore ideal for the wine lover with limited cellar space as there are no tannins to soften with age, and the wines are very drinkable within one to two years, but will also keep for ten years. Having compared and enjoyed these wines at home it was only natural that we should call to restock when next in the area. We re-visited this Summer, but the Coopérative was closed for a stock-take, on a Saturday, at 4.00pm, who would have believed it! No amount of pleading, that we had travelled all the way from England, no amount of flattery, would change Madame's mind. I was gutted! I now know how children feel when they throw their toys out of the cot!

Looking hurriedly at the map we noticed that the wine village of Paziols was nearby, and knowing from our research that the Coopérative in Paziols produced quality Fitou and Rivesaltes, we overcame our disappointment and headed for Paziols. We had earlier that week purchased and enjoyed a Fitou, 'Cuvée Sainte Anne', produced in Paziols, from one of the large supermarkets, and it was only proper that we should mention this to the man at the Coopérative. He was not impressed! Apparently, they produce bulk blends for the big buyers, but he obviously did not rate the wine, and was most dismissive of it. He said the wine was even inferior to their basic Fitou Sélection. He was right, Fitou Sélection was far superior! However from their range we preferred the dark, solid, mature fruitiness of the four year old wine produced from a 60/40 grape blend from 40 year old Carignan and Grenache vines, aged in oak for 18 months, a gorgeous, intense strong red. When we drink this wine at home, we give thanks to Madame at Latour de France, and her stock-take, without which, we would not have stumbled on this fabulous Fitou!

We were then treated to a range of wonderful Rivesaltes and particularly enjoyed the intensely perfumed Muscat de Rivesaltes. We purchased a couple of bottles, one of which we will savour with *foie gras d'oie* (purchased from a producer, at the picturesque market in Sarlat, during an earlier holiday in the Périgord) during a special meal to celebrate the new Millenium.

For those with a geological interest in weathered rock formations, a visit to the 'Orgues', near to the village of Ille-sur-Tête is fascinating. Eerie columns of rock, often 50-60 feet high, stand in groups like prehistoric statues, but these have been produced by erosion, not by man. They are neither on the scale of the rock columns in Bryce Canyon nor the Utah rock bluffs in America, but are none-the-less, very interesting.

Whilst in the area, a trip to the picturesque hill village of Castelnou is a must. We arrived mid-morning, it was hot, still and deathly quiet. We walked into Castelnou, a walled feudal village, and sat for a few minutes, in the square by the post office, absorbing the heavenly atmosphere. It was so peaceful, I had to check if my watch had stopped! Spiritually refreshed, we set off up the cobbled path, on stones rounded and polished by countless generations of Catalan farmers, wine growers, Cathars, Crusaders and more recently by retired city dwellers seeking, finding and enjoying the beauty and tranquillity of the Haut Languedoc. Onwards and upwards, between and round the ancient houses, to the restored 10th century keep and a rewarding panorama of the wooded hilly countryside.

We could smell the country freshness and garlic and rosemary and thyme and cooking! Noses twitching, we were drawn to a small restaurant and enjoyed a lazy Catalan lunch, washed down with a robust red from St. Chinian, on the restaurant terrace high in the old village, yes, definitely on the visitor's 'must visit' list.

The warmth and stillness was still in evidence that night eating on the terrace back at the hotel. The murmur of contented diners, the sparkling glasses reflecting the flickering candles, the mixed aromas of well prepared food, the soft, tasteful guitar music, a truly romantic occasion was suddenly shattered. A large dog, and I mean a large dog, up until that time sprawled like a deep pile rug next to its master, suddenly espied the head of a tiny dog peeping over the rim of a well-dressed, elderly lady's hand bag, three tables away. The big dog growled, standing up to its full height, pulled at its lead, which had been wrapped around the owners chair leg, decanted the owner on the floor, who swore (at least I think he swore) lunged for the lead and managed to restrain his dog in time to prevent any carnage. Meanwhile the little dog had shrieked, and with a backwards somersault, dived trembling, back into the handbag. The elderly lady jumped to her feet, shouted and swore at the big dog's owner, the gist of her outburst being, " Why don't you keep that hairy monster of yours under control, my little 'Fifi' almost died of fright." After which, she picked up her handbag and stormed off to her room, cooing sympathetically to 'Fifi' en route. Her husband who had sat silently through this episode, picked up his glass and smiled. The big dog owner marched his dog back to his room. Within seconds the diners' murmurings recommenced and the restaurant was once again back to normal.

The French are extremely tolerant diners especially with children, animals, and smokers. We admire their tolerance of children, as it is perfectly natural for families to eat together. In all our travels in France, children are always welcomed by restaurant staff and diners, and we have never seen children misbehaving. Knowing of the French love affair with animals, especially dogs, one can understand their tolerance of dogs, but as for smokers, we cannot understand why the French, who enjoy food, are so tolerant of them. Being reformed smokers, the Browns along with many diners in the UK, prefer non-smoking restaurants, after all, smell and taste, as with wine, play significant roles in the enjoyment of food.

For families with young children the beaches are excellent, there are almost 100 km. of sandy beaches, most of which are clean and guarded. Washed by the gentler Mediterranean Sea, swimming is more enjoyable than in the bone-shattering breakers of the Atlantic found on a similar expanse of beach on the west coast from Soulac to Biarritz. Although this coast is a very popular holiday area, with such an expanse of sand, it is rarely as crowded as other beaches in the south of France. This area also has the advantage of having good honest wines close at hand. The holiday resorts are less spectacular than La Grande Motte, with conventional low rise properties bordering the seashore. Of interest are the old fishermen's timber chalets built on stilts in the town of Gruissan, which are now enclosed in a large estate of look-alike properties, and are a complete contrast to the imitation 'Moorish'-style apartments bordering the more affluent marina complex in the new town area of Gruissan. Further south the Pyrenees dominate the background and the coastline becomes more rugged.

The beaches at Collioure and Banyuls, are at a premium, but rock pools abound for inquisitive children seeking sea anemones, fish, hermit crabs and shrimps. These towns are still active fishing ports, bringing in their sought after catches of anchovies, a great delicacy of the area. Collioure, in the height of Summer is very popular, especially at weekends, and parking can be difficult. But it should not be missed, and it is easy to see why over the years many famous artists have been drawn to the old town, the dominating castle, the brightly painted boats, eager to put on canvas the added warmth of colours enhanced by the intensity and clarity of light which this area enjoys.

Inland from Narbonne, after crossing the River Aude and the Canal du Midi, the countryside becomes more rugged as one follows the rivers upstream. The ancient stronghold of Minerve sits atop of a ridge where the Briant joins the Cesse, which ultimately flows into the River Aude below St. Marcel. The view from the approach road is spectacular and it is easy to see why Minerve was able to resist many invading hordes, until it inevitably surrendered to Simon de Montfort in 1209 when, in retribution, 140 heretics were burned. This ancient town gives its name to one of the regions greatest wines, Minervois, and some of the better wines are grown around the town. We stopped, tasted, and purchased wine from one of the growers in this area and enjoyed the deep dark red, with its clean berry and plummy flavours. These wines with 60% Syrah, gained greater complexity when aged in oak for 6 months. Our final verdict a good clean balanced drinking wine. The lighter wine had been named by the wine grower after the young daughter of his oenologist, demonstrating the respect given to the genius of the man without whom the wine would be destined for the 'wine lake'.

This homage to the wine maker does not stop at wine, I recall on a separate occasion in Charente, we visited the house of Hennessey, in Cognac, and found that the most revered person in the company was the 'magician' who selected and blended the *'eau de vie'* to make the cognac, and, that the current incumbent was from the ninth generation!

Further north is the region of St. Chinian, where fruity spicy wines are produced from a blend of Syrah, Grenache and Carignan grapes. Being produced from grapes grown at a slightly higher altitude, the wines are less 'up front' and more elegant than those of the Languedoc plain. The oak aged wine from the Coopérative in St. Chinian is a good example and will be enjoyed by the Browns, with roasts, on many a Winter's night.

If one continues in a north-westerly direction, the hairpins increase and vines are replaced first by timber in the Montagnes Noires, then once through the mountain by sunflowers and maize until after Castres, one reaches the medieval village of Lautrec, a pretty unspoilt town with many half-timbered houses, but alas, no wine! However to all lovers of French cuisine, this place is a must. Lautrec is the home of probably the best garlic in the World, 'Ail Rose de Lautrec.' The Browns have bought Rose Lautrec garlic on many occasions, from several Provençal markets and enjoyed its superior flavour and good keeping qualities compared to ordinary French garlic. As for garlic purchased from UK supermarkets, there is no comparison! The garlic growers of Lautrec market over 4,000 tonnes a year of garlic, 10% of all garlic grown in France, and hold a garlic festival each August, where visitors are treated too, amongst other things, garlic soup! What would we do without garlic; *escargots, moules,* and salads would not taste the same, and we would probably be over-run with vampires. Perish the thought!

The only problem with garlic is that although it is enjoyable to the eater, it doesn't necessarily give pleasure to one's companion either at the time or even the following day. To overcome this problem one is advised to follow the garlic meal with raw parsley, but have you ever tried eating raw parsley?!

Returning to wine after this gastronomic episode, the other quality reds in the Languedoc, besides those of St. Chinian are from Faugères. From grapes grown in the foothills of the Cévennes, adjacent to the St. Chinian vineyards, the seven communes of Faugères produce full bodied, rich dark ruby coloured, fine fruity wines. The best of these wines based on Cinsault are produced when the percentage of Carignan is partially, or totally, replaced by Syrah, Mourvèdre and Grenache. Of these wines, those lovingly produced at the Château de Grézan, near Laurens, take some beating.

As I have mentioned previously, our interest in this region of France was first aroused by a range of good Midi wines from 'Bottoms Up' and Faugères, from Château de Laurens, was one of these. It transpires that this wine is now produced at the nearby Château de Grézan, apparently three of the best growers in the region have pooled their expertise, one concentrating on growing vines, one on making wine and one on marketing. Of these three, the expertise on making the wine lies with Château Grézan, and do they know how to make wine!

The quality increases from the good Château de Laurens and the similar Château Grézan Genérique to the better Château Grézan Cuvée Arnaud Lubac, to the sublime Château Grézan Vielles Vignes. A memorable tasting, in this walled restored Templar fortress (a little like Aigues-Mortes but on a smaller scale) will always be recalled when opening a bottle back home.

The largest of the wine appellations in this region is Corbières, and one of the best Corbières is produced by Château de Lastours near the A9, *La Languedocienne*, 12 km. from Sigean. We have bought and enjoyed wine from Château de Lastours, purchased from supermarkets in the UK, so being in the area we decided to visit the Château. As we arrived, a gruff South Yorkshire voice greeted us. "Damn good wine here, I always stop and buy from Lastours, best wine in Corbières" he said, as he carefully packed cases in his caravan. Not all the wine experts live in the Home Counties, I thought. We entered the cool tasting room and enjoyed not only the UK supermarket grade, but their range of superior wines, including a glorious 14.1% rich, dark, tannic wine and one with great potential to reach maturity well into the next century, simply labelled Château Lastours, whose quality was reflected in its price of £11 per bottle. At the end of the tasting, there was no question in our minds, the chap from Barnsley was right, "Best wine in Corbières!" Whilst we were savouring a second glass of the top wine, a young, flushed, excited couple entered, who, it transpired, were discussing the arrangements for their wedding reception with Madame. What a place for a reception! "Can we get married again, darling?" I mused.

With a half full load of wine we set off for the Vaucluse and an appointment with our favourite vigneron in Rasteau.

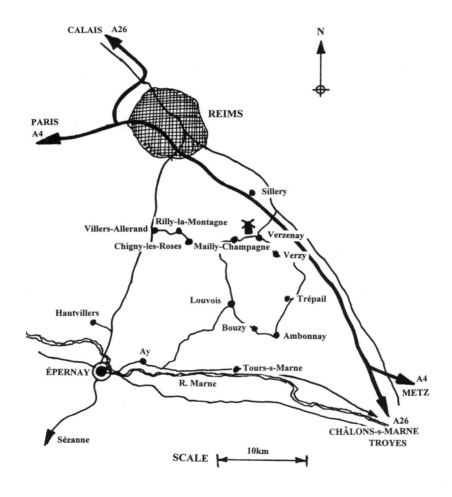

# 12

## Bubbles and Babies.

There is only one Champagne, but there are many excellent pretenders.

It is the intention in this chapter to demonstrate to the wine lover who has also a penchant for champagne that good champagne can be obtained at reasonable prices from the smaller producers in the Champagne region, and also, that there are many sparkling wines, more often than not produced by the *méthode champenoise* which compare favourably to champagne in quality, whilst meeting the key requirement of the wine drinker, value for money!

In the late 17th Century, Dom Pérignon, the blind cellarmaster, at the Benedictine abbey in Hautvillers, a hillside village near Épernay, is reputed to have produced the first champagne. I say reputed, because sparkling wine had been produced in the area, for many years. Wine produced after the harvest contained residual yeast and sugars which in the warmth of the following year started a second fermentation producing carbon dioxide which was either retained in the bottle by the stopper producing a semi-sparkling wine, or, escaped through the stopper producing a slightly more alcoholic flat wine, or occasionally, caused bottles to explode. I suspect that with many northern wines, even in Tudor England, when sugar was added to reduce the acidity and increase the alcohol content, the wine, if left in the cellar for a time, would have produced a petulant, or even sparkling wine.

I recall, as a lad, making rose hip syrup, and one day finding an exploded jar under the stairs, a strong sweet alcoholic smell and a well sprayed wall. Obviously yeast from the rose hips had reacted with the sugar to produce alcoholic, sparkling rose hip syrup.

Needless to say, having to clear up the sticky mess cured me of further attempts at rose hip syrup! I suppose in a way I had stumbled on secondary fermentation, but 300 years after Dom Pérignon.

Whether Dom Pérignon actually produced the first champagne is not important, what he did was to make clear wine, add sugar and cork the bottle, design a safer bottle, and produce the forerunner of present day champagne.

To commemorate his achievement a statue has been erected in the grounds of the largest champagne producer, Moët et Chandon, at their world famous Maison de Champagne in Épernay. A more humble memorial, is the gravestone, in the church near the Abbey in Hautvillers. Moët et Chandon, as a lasting tribute to this great man, name and market their top brand champagne, as Dom Pérignon. This is a truly great Champagne, and a memorable drink, but because of its high price, its appearance in the Brown household is limited to very special occasions. Having tasted and enjoyed Dom Pérignon it is not surprising that the wine lover should search for a cheaper alternative.

If the reader wishes to buy champagne at lower prices than are available in the UK, pop over to France, but ignore the 'Duty-free'. The supermarket 'Leclerc' at Outreau, outside Boulogne has probably one of the widest selections and at good prices, where savings of 30-50% on UK prices can be made. However if you really want to buy champagne and savour the memory of the tasting and purchase, the reader should visit the Champagne region.

To gain an understanding of Champagne and the champagne process an organised trip around one of the Champagne Houses in Épernay is well worth the visit. At Moët et Chandon, in the foyer, there is a display of magnums of champagne, autographed by Formula 1 racing drivers recording the long term relationship between Moët et Chandon and motor racing. A guided tour costing 20 francs, is very interesting and informative.

The guide gives a potted history of the company from its founding in 1743 to the current day where it now forms part of the LVMH Group along with Hennessey cognac. The tour then proceeds through part of the 18 miles of underground cellars, past millions of bottles of champagne undergoing secondary fermentation or resting (the money tied up in stock must be mind boggling). Non-vintage champagne must remain in this condition for 12 months and vintage champagne for a minimum of 36 months before the sediment is removed. The tour continues past rows and rows of wooden *pupitres*, where the sediment is encouraged to collect at the neck by gradually inverting and part-rotating the bottles over a 6 week period. This process is called *'remuage'* and a team of *'remuers'* are permanently employed to carry out this important operation. A little like painting the Forth bridge I thought, once you've finished, it's time to start again! The next stage is the *dégorgement* when the neck of the bottle is frozen by immersion in cold brine solution at -25°C and the top seal, and the plug of ice containing the sediment, are removed. The champagne is then topped up with a sweet liqueur of cane sugar in champagne and the bottle corked. After a further period in storage the champagne is labelled and given its characteristic foil wrapping. The strength of sugar in the added liqueur determines whether the champagne is *'brut'*, 'extra dry', *'sec'* or *'demi-sec'*. The tour finally ends in the tasting room where the visitor can enjoy a glass of champagne, but unfortunately, not 'Dom Pérignon'!

On one such visit, the guide who spoke perfect English, enthused and waxed lyrical about his beloved nectar but at one point brought a smile to my face. He was explaining that in the process there is a slight sediment in the wine, called 'feet.' Strange I thought. It then dawned on me, from my days as an industrial chemist, I recalled that oils frequently had a deposit and this is called 'foots.' Our guide in his attempt at perfect English had converted 'foots' to 'feet,' hence my smile. Fortunately he didn't see my face as we were in a darkened storage alley at the time, an explanation could have proved difficult, if not embarrassing.

During the tour one is told that wines from 3 grapes are used in champagne, Chardonnay, Pinot Noir and Pinot Meunier. Of these grapes Pinot Noir and Pinot Meunier are both black skinned, but only the grape juice is used, otherwise the colour of the skins would colour the champagne. Depending on the producer, pink champagne (rosé) is produced by either adding a little red wine or by allowing infusion of colour from the grape skins. After the tasting, the tour finishes in the factory shop, where the range of Moët et Chandon champagnes can be purchased at good prices. They also sell an own-brand very useful bottle opener!

Visits can be made to other major Champagne Houses, one even has a small tourist train to transport visitors through its cellars! Equipped with a limited knowledge of champagne the visitor is now ready to seek out his or her own specialist champagne producer. The major Champagne Houses because of the enormous volumes used, supplement their own grapes with grapes from growers in the 3 regions of Champagne, Montagne de Reims, Vallée de la Marne and Côte des Blancs. The prices paid for the grapes are dependant on quality, Grand Cru growers get the best prices, Premier Cru producers the next, etc. Champagne produced from these grapes can be called Grand Cru and Premier Cru respectively, and this wording normally appears on labels of the smaller champagne producers. These are the champagnes that will appeal to the wine drinker, the quality is invariably good, and because the producers do not have to carry the marketing and promotional costs of the large producers, they are able to sell their champagne at reasonable prices. After all, to the wine drinker price is very important!

After Épernay, the visitor in a hurry, must visit Reims. It is not only the capital of the region, but also has one of the finest cathedrals in the whole of France. In the square, facing the cathedral, the tourist information office is to the left, and close by, on the corner of the square, a *'Maison de Champagne'*, where numerous makes and varieties of champagne can be purchased.

For the visitor with more time to spare than a whistle-stop tour, the tourist information centre in Reims should be the first port of call. It has a wealth of information on the region and champagne.

Last year, on a visit, to introduce my sister and *beau-frère* to Champagne, we picked up a leaflet advertising a *'Fête du Goût'* in one of the champagne villages, Chigny-les-Roses. It was the village's first *'Fête du Goût'* and, it was that weekend! Not surprisingly, our planned itinerary had to be adjusted to fit in a visit to Chigny-les-Roses!

The following morning, the Sun was shining, not a bad day for mid-October, and a glorious day to visit Chigny-les-Roses. We meandered through the vineyards of the Montagne de Reims, through Verzenay, past the windmill, through Mailly-Champagne and Ludes to Chigny-les-Roses. The village is classified as a Premier Cru village and champagne produced from the grapes is Premier Cru champagne.

As we approached the village of approximately 60 houses, we were directed to the *Salle des Fêtes* and passed several houses with *'Accueil'fanions* (welcome pennants). We parked the car and entered the village hall, it was deserted, we were obviously the first visitors that day. We were greeted by one of the viticulteurs, who welcomed us to the village, and provided general information on the village and a map with 20 houses listed who would welcome visitors to taste their champagnes and in certain cases would provide portions of local food. These houses would all display the *'Accueil'* pennants. My sister was 'gob-smacked', she couldn't believe that on her first visit to Champagne that she could taste up to 50 champagnes, for free!

Our genial host explained that wines were produced from 3 types of grape and invited us to taste samples of the 3 fresh wines. We were surprised with the dryness and acidity of the wines, in fact I would have called them thin. I then recalled that in the Loire, if the growing season has been poor, rather than make inferior Vouvray or Saumur wines, the vignerons divert the wine to make sparkling wine. So, is this the reason why champagne is almost exclusively produced here in this most northerly vineyard in France, and why the vignerons having accepted that the champagne is superior to still wine, have concentrated on developing and marketing the best sparkling wine in the world, Champagne!

Back to the wines, the Chardonnay tasted of fresh dry apples and vanilla, the Pinot Noir of exotic dry spicy fruits and the Meunier of currants with a hint of liquorice. It was when the wines were blended in approximately equal proportions that a more balanced wine with enhanced flavours was produced. The viticulteur said in his champagne he used a greater percentage of Chardonnay, but that was his preference and other producers would use different proportions in their champagnes. We thanked him for insight into the art of the vigneron and set off for the village square.

As is normal practise we bought tasting glasses engraved with Chigny-les-Roses and set off for our first taste.

Our first taste was in a Tixier house, our second taste was in another Tixier house and our fifth tasting was in yet another Tixier house. In all there were 4 Tixier vignerons in the village, all male. My sister, 'an equal rights for women campaigner', with a degree of Dutch courage, courtesy of the champagne, asked in faltering French, "Why is it that all the Tixier champagnes are prefixed with male Christian names, why are there no female names?"

M. Tixier shrugged his shoulders and replied, "It is very simple, men make champagne, women make babies!" I've never laughed as much for a long time!

M.Tixier's comment reminded me of the time we stayed in a ferme-auberge in Savoie. We had arrived from the south with a boot full of wine which Monsieur, the farmer allowed me to store in his spacious larder. As I carefully laid the last case, I saw drops of blood on my arm, I thought it is warm and I have been working hard, but surely not sweating blood! With relief I noticed that the blood was from two hanging rabbits (tomorrow's dinner no doubt.) This was indeed the case.

As I was unloading the boot I noticed a shaven-headed tattooed man in a vest watching me from the first floor balcony. At dinner there were 11 other guests, a French couple and their two sons, a young French couple, the shaven-headed tattooed man with his wife and young daughter, a Scottish couple and the Browns. Dinner was good, farmhouse cooking, prepared by Madame, which we ate together at a long farmhouse table. As the meal progressed, our first and most memorable *raclette*, and as the wine flowed, we introduced ourselves. We were the mad English who liked wine, the Scots were in Savoie for the walking, the French couple with two sons, all wearing woollen jerseys were from Paris on route to the Adriatic, the tattooed man was on holiday from Marseille and the young couple, from Normandy, were on a return holiday. I sat next to the man from Marseille, and amongst other things we discussed during dinner were the merits of pastis, and I was assured that there is only one pastis, Ricard. If I am ever asked on which pastis to drink, I now quote the man from Marseille.

We were now into our fourth or fifth glass of wine, and the conversation drifted onto children, our two were married, the Scots had one at university, the Parisian's sons were at junior school, and the man from Marseille's daughter was the youngest of four and was also at junior school. The young couple had a little boy, of 18 months, who was back at home being looked after by grandmother whilst they were on holiday. She was a very pretty girl with waist length ginger hair and a pale freckled complexion and was more comfortable speaking in English than her husband. She spoke in faltering English and blushing said that she and her husband were on holiday to make babies! Whereupon the man from Marseille leapt to his feet and offered his services to help make babies. The place erupted!

Still chuckling at M. Tixier's comments, and recalling the man from Marseille, we called on Jany Roupsy and enjoyed champagne Gil Roupsy, especially the *brut* 'Blanc de Blancs', and a plate of hot tasty cheese and onion savouries prepared by his wife, Nadine. Excellent!

**Vineyards of Montagne de Reims near Verzenay.**

Walking down the street, glasses in hand, we met a man from Mailly-Champagne, a Grand Cru village, who was also tasting champagne. We discussed the merits of the various champagnes, and agreed they were very good and at prices of 70-80 francs a bottle, very good value. We mentioned that we particularly enjoy the Mailly Grand Cru 'Cuvée des Echansons', which in our opinion, with its elegant almond, honey spice flavour, is as good as the best of the major Champagne Houses vintage champagne. He nodded his approval, and went on to say that he also produced good, inexpensive champagne in Mailly, and invited us to their *'Foire'* which is held over 3 days at the end of May each year. We made a mental note to visit in May.

Feeling peckish, we retraced our steps back to the square, purchased bread, local goat's cheese, rabbit and duck terrine, and drinks from the market stalls, and settled down on the church steps to enjoy a well-earned picnic in the warm October sunshine. We all agreed that this was a perfect way to spend a Sunday morning.

Sitting on the church steps, reflecting in the warmth of the Sun, my mind wandered to a hot July day in a similar sized village to the north west of Limoges in Haute-Vienne, but that was not a happy place. In that village, nothing moved, the air was hot and still, no birds sang, it was the village of Oradour-sur-Glane. Up until 10 June 1944, it had been a happy village, but on that day, four days after the Allies landed in Normandy, in an act of revenge, the German SS systematically massacred the 642 villagers, including 207 children and ransacked the village. The village has been maintained as the Germans left it, as a memorial to man's inhumanity to man. Near the village green, where the Germans held their roll call, is an underground memorial where all the murdered villagers' names are listed.

Reading through the lists was so heart-wrenching. Whole families died that day, grandparents, parents, brothers, sisters, aunts and uncles, children as young as 3 months, and no doubt several unborn children. It is probably the saddest place in France, a most moving experience. They have rebuilt a new Oradour, approximately half a mile away, whose council, out of respect, still insist, after more than 50 years, that villagers paint their shutters grey. We purchased a small book in the village, which we feel should be read by leaders of any country contemplating acts of aggression against another country. Anne asked me why I was so quiet, "I was just remembering Oradour." She held my hand and gently brought me back to Chigny-les-Roses.

It wasn't long before other families joined the Browns, on the church steps for lunch. Our discussion, on the preference for soft fresh or hard mature goat's cheese was interrupted by a slowly moving procession of colourful, highly polished, open-topped Classic Porches, which drew up in the square. The drivers strolled round the square, chatted, posed by their vehicles, and then, after a few minutes, with horns blaring, drove off. Within minutes the peace in the square was shattered by the noise of an approaching army of sewing machines, and a convoy of gleaming 2CV's appeared, and as suddenly, (if that is the right word when describing the motion of 2CV's) disappeared. We really did appreciate the *'Fête'* organisers arranging such a welcome for the Browns' first visit to Chigny-les-Roses.

That night over an excellent meal, with champagne of course, in the 'Relais de Sillery', we voted the day a great success and a memorable first visit to Champagne for my sister and *beau-frère.*

All the villages in the region are involved in champagne, and many houses in each village produce and sell champagne. As most Frenchmen have their own pet champagne supplier, it is only natural for Francophiles to have their own supplier. The Browns' favourite comes from the Grand Cru village of Sillery, which being on the plain on the edge of the Montagne de Reims, has a second industry, sugar beet and a 'Begin Say' sugar refinery. Not only does it have one of the best restaurants in the area, but in François Secondé, one of the best champagne producers. His Grand Cru Sillery *brut* and his rosé are simply sublime.

While in the area the wine drinker should visit Bouzy, one of the few places in the Champagne region to produce a still wine. This red Bouzy is produced from Pinot Noir, but is a lightweight fruity wine compared to the blockbusters from Burgundy. The 'St. Vincent' restaurant in the next village, Ambonnay, serves quality regional food, and should not be missed by the diner seeking to savour the flavours of the region.

Enough of Champagne, now to the pretenders. Down in the South of France, between Carcassonne and the Pyrenees is the town of Limoux, whose main claim to fame is that sparkling wine was discovered in their Abbaye de Saint-Hilaire, before Dom Pérignon in Hautvillers. Being a romantic at heart, I tend to favour the blind monk in Hautvillers who was reputed to have imagined his champagne to wine filled with 'twinkling, bursting stars' as being the discoverer of champagne.

In Limoux, sparkling wine was originally produced from the Mauzac grape, but to build in the right level of acidity and sharpness the grapes were harvested in an unripe condition. More recently the producers have been permitted to use Chenin Blanc and Chardonnay grapes, and in their Crémant de Limoux produce good honest sparklers which at their best compare favourably with Loire sparklers.

In our travels we have tasted many inexpensive sparkling wines, but find that the ones produced in the south, tend to lack the sharpness of their northern cousins, probably because of the use of ripe grapes, so we believe that for a pretender to be taken seriously, the producer must use under-ripe grapes or grapes known to produce wines with an acidic character.

From our experiences we have split the pretenders into two categories, 'bubbly' and 'serious'.

'Bubbly' pretenders are good honest sparklers, not too complex in flavour with little after-taste (referred to, by our children when younger, as 'happy juice') party drinks, not to be seriously savoured but ideal for a romantic picnic on a warm Summer's afternoon. Picture the scene, a hot July day, in the dappled shade of a large weeping willow, by the side of lazy river in the heart of the English countryside, with an attractive member of the opposite sex, a picnic of strawberries and cream and several glasses of chilled bubbly, yes!

There are many sparklers in this category, one of our favourites from Duras mentioned in Chapter 3, Clairette de Die from the Drôme, Seyssel from Savoie (especially the Royal Seyssel produced by Varichon and Clerc), the afore mentioned sparklers from Limoux, Crémants d'Alsace, and the lower priced sparklers of Vouvray and Saumur. There is a considerable choice of sparklers available on the market and as wine lovers our advice to the reader would be to buy a selection from a French supermarket and find one's own 'bubbly'.

'Serious' pretenders are the better quality Vouvrays, Saumurs, Crémants de Loire and the Crémants de Bourgogne. I have mentioned the Vouvrays, Saumurs and the Crémants de Loire in Chapter 9 and the best of these are indeed serious competitors to non-vintage champagne, and the presence of several of the well known Champagne Houses in the area can only enhance their reputation further. Crémants de Bourgogne from Lugny and Viré in the Mâconnais are very good, but in our opinion the best Crémant de Bourgogne is produced in the underground caves at Bailly near Auxerre.

This serious pretender is produced by the Coopérative, SICAVA de Bailly but only since its formation in 1972. Before that date, after the Second World War, the white wine of the region was in great demand as a base wine by Champagne shippers and by German Sekt sparkling wine producers. But as with most things, all good things eventually come to an end. In this case as the Champagne and Sekt producers became self sufficient, the demand for this wine diminished.

The white wine producers met, scratched their heads, and formed the Coopérative on the basis that if their white wine was good enough to be made into Champagne and Sekt, why shouldn't they make it themselves! What a good decision this has turned out to be!

The visitor drives into the cave, parks the vehicle and crosses to a brightly lit semi-circular bar where one can taste their remarkable range of non-vintage and vintage Crémants, the best of which are sold under the 'Meurgis' label. Very good, and serious competition to champagne, with the added bonus of being half the price! They also produce Sauvignon St. Bris, Bourgogne Aligoté and Bourgogne Rouge and a comprehensive range of crèmes (Cassis, Framboise, Mure, Cerise and Pêche) but these are mainly as a sideline to their Crémant production. On one occasion as we stood at the bar discussing the merits of two vintages, we were asked if we would like a tour of their caves, by would you believe it, a second Auntie Frances! I could not believe it, either Granddad had had secret liaisons in France, or a much travelled 'Johnny Onion' had dallied awhile in Lancashire! The tour was similar to, but less grand, than that at Moët et Chandon, and ended with a glass of 'Meurgis'.

As proof of the quality of this exceptional Crémant de Bourgogne, we organised copious quantities of vintage 'Meurgis' to be served throughout our daughter's wedding. What a day and what a night! On a warm Summer's day, walking on the lawns and through the gardens of a country house, chatting with friends and relatives, watching a game of serious croquet, with the laughter of children in the background, having empty glasses replaced by further full glasses of 'Meurgis' by attentive waitresses, while the beautiful couple and their attendants were being photographed in the flower garden, how proud we felt, as would our parents have been, had they still been alive. A perfect day! During the day and the evening, many of the guests said how much they had enjoyed 'real' champagne, with taste and body, rather than the bland champagne normally served at weddings.

As Cheryl and John departed for their Caribbean honeymoon, the sight of so many laughing happy people brought to mind the children's description of bubbly as 'happy juice'. It is amazing how perceptive young children can be!

A final experience with champagne. The majority of

champagne producers say that once non-vintage champagne is bottled it should be drunk within 1-2 years, as it will not improve with keeping and may in fact lose its 'fizz'. Perhaps this is a marketing ploy to persuade purchasers to drink rather than store champagne, and thereby increase their champagne sales.

Last year we opened a jeroboam of non-vintage white foil 'Pol Roger', which must have been bottled at least 15 years ago. This bottle had followed the Browns through 3 house moves, was always stored vertically in a cool darkened space, (usually under the stairs) and was being kept for a special family occasion.

Last year we opened the bottle at a close family celebration of the birth of our first grandchild, Matthew Finn, and the champagne was brilliant, full of bubbles and oodles of yeasty mellow fruits, with the beneficial roundness of its long time in bottle. The perfect way to welcome the next generation of Brown wine lovers! The moral being, don't believe everything marketing people say!

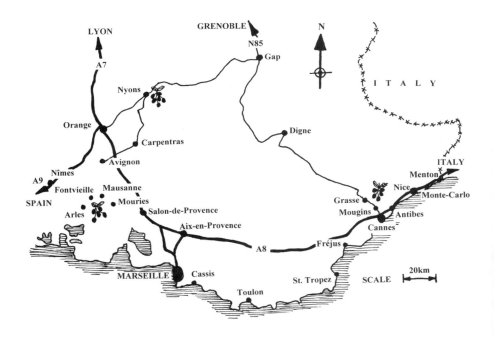

# 13

# Olive Oil, the alternative wine.

Being committed Francophiles, it is not surprising that during our travels we have stumbled across that fruity golden-green liquid, the alternative wine, olive oil. Not that mass produced bland supermarket oil, but the liquid sunshine from Provence, 100% natural, cold pressed, extra virgin olive oil, free from added chemicals or preservatives.

It is now possible to purchase a wide range of olive oils in the UK, a far cry from days, not too long ago, when without specialist shops the only place to purchase olive oil was in high street chemists. Yes things have certainly improved for the better! Over the past few years UK supermarkets have increased their range of oils from Spain, Greece and Italy, especially Tuscany, but very rarely does one come across Provençal olive oil. Why? Come to think of it, one very rarely comes across Provençal olive oil in French supermarkets!

The answer is probably price, as Provençal oil, like quality Tuscan oil is three or four times as expensive as ordinary olive oil, and therefore outside the price range which supermarket customers are perceived as willing to pay. As with quality wine, you either buy from a wine merchant or from the vigneron direct.

This last point was brought home to the Browns, one night in the Vaucluse, the night of the Sablet Grand Ball. We were enjoying our second cool beer, when a Belgian sat down at our table. Overhearing our English, he started up a conversation. He was down in the Vaucluse with his family, combining a holiday with a property search and would be soon departing for Provence. Not surprising, it wasn't long before the subject of wine was raised, and in particular the pearl of the Vaucluse, Gigondas. We discussed the merits of various producers, and although we put up a strong case for several including Raspail Ay, he was adamant that the best Gigondas was 'Domaine du Pesquier' produced by the Boutiere family. (We have since compared it to other Gigondas and yes it is good, but the best, we doubt it.) Bearing in mind the number of producers and the variation in different vintages we doubt if even an expert could get any closer than selecting a top five.

We mentioned our liking for Beaujolais wines and in particular Juliénas. He was most dismissive of these wines saying that the only decent wine came from north of Beaune! What a self opinionated person, I thought, I bet he's never tried Daniel's Juliénas!

We changed the subject to food, restaurants and eventually olive oil and how widely it was used in Provence. "Not surprising," I said, "considering the low price of oil such as 'Puget' in the supermarkets." "Puget, huh, *pour la voiture*," he snorted, "the only good oil comes from Provence." His eyes glazed and in a calmer voice, went on to explain that his real reason for going to Provence was to exchange a case of 'Gevrey-Chambertin' which he had purchased on his way down, for ten litres of oil from his 'olive man' in Provence. I nearly asked him if it was for his motor car, but decided against it. We gently questioned him but he would not disclose his supplier.

That night reflecting on the day, and our conversation with the Belgian we decided that we would find our own 'olive man'!

The Mediterranean climate enjoyed in the south of France and in Provence in particular encouraged the Greeks to introduce olives to the region over 2,500 years ago. Whether olives preceded grapes is of historical interest only, the fact is that both fruits have thrived and prospered and with their acceptance as healthy foods by the medical profession have an unlimited future in this climate. There are many similarities between grape vines and olive trees, both thrive in poor soil, both produce fruit which are eaten as fruit or are pressed to release juices, beneficial to humans. There are many varieties, from those which are picked in an un-ripened state in the Alpilles, to fruit which are left on the tree until fully ripe as the Tanche olive near Nyons, imparting a fresh 'green' flavour or a ripe golden fruity flavour to the olives or the olive oil respectively. With such variety and with the Brown's appetite well and truly whetted by the Belgian the search commenced.

Reading through our literature, and local information collected from tourist information offices, we decided that the olive capital of the Vaucluse, Nyons (actually located in Drôme) should be our first port of call. Nyons is not only the most northerly region for olives, but it is unique in being the only area in France granted the *Appellation d'origine Contrôlée* for its olives and its olive oil. We called at the Coopérative in Nyons and were amazed at the variety of products manufactured from the humble olive. Pride of place went to the cold-pressed Extra Virgin Olive Oil, which was available in various sizes of bottles and cans, but all at a price of about 100-120 francs per litre. "More than I'd pay for good wine," I said to Anne. "But, Bob this is the equivalent in oil of First Cru Bordeaux!" she replied. Putting it that way, how could I object to a few litres of oil! Next the olives, probably the best, most succulent fleshy olives in France, and freely available to taste. They were gorgeous! Two kg. of vacuum packed and bottled olives joined the oil in our trolley. Whilst Anne was considering the purchase of *tapenade* my mind drifted back to our first tasting of the *olives noires de Nyons*.

It was the day of the *Fête du Truffe* in a small village to the north of Suze-la-Rousse. It was one hot Sunday morning in late August. The village was certainly *'en fête,'* bunting was everywhere, canned music was playing over the loudspeakers and the square and side roads were lined with stalls, selling anything from freshly baked bread and pastries to antiques. We followed the crowd and came upon a drinks stall selling *'tomate'* and *'miro'*. Feeling a trifle parched we succumbed to a *'tomate'* (Ricard, Evian water and

Grenadine) at 6 francs a glass, and were offered *olives noires de Nyons*. A very tasty combination, and worthy of a second helping, but this time the olives were coated in *'Herbes de Provence.'* It was difficult to say which combination we preferred, so surprise, surprise, we had another *'tomate.'* To this day I am still undecided whether it was the olives or the *'tomate'* that made such a memorable aperitif.

"Should we buy *tapenade* as part of a holiday present for Pauline and Kath?" Anne asked. "What?" I replied. " Where were you, dear? Dreaming again, no doubt!" I said, "I was just remembering that day drinking *'tomate'* at the truffle fair and eating those juicy rich dark Nyons olives."

"Wasn't that the time when we saw the old man dressed as Toulouse Lautrec, gingerly weaving his way through the crowds on his tricycle whilst playing his accordian?" asked Anne. "Yes, it was, and until we saw that he was controlling the direction of the tricycle with a tiller between his knees we thought we'd drunk too much *'tomate'*!" I replied.

Anne decided to buy some jars of *tapenade* and then wandered off to seek out other olive products. I helped myself to a few more tasty olives and cast my mind back to the *Fête du Truffe*. Suitably refreshed we arrived at the truffle stall and joined the queue for truffle omelettes. There were four ladies in the truffle team. One broke and whisked two to three dozen eggs in a large bowl. A second lady added slivers of truffle to the whisked eggs by holding the truffle and scraping with a potato peeler, had it not been for the faint fungal smell, she could have been peeling potatoes! A third lady oiled a frying pan with sunflower oil and poured a ladle of truffle and egg mixture into the smoking pan, and within less than a minute decanted a well rolled moist omelette onto the fourth lady's plate, followed by a piece of fresh baguette, and cutlery. All for 30 francs! As is often the case some people try and jump the queue, I resisted one pushy person, until I calculated that he would receive less truffles in his omelette, at which time I graciously allowed him to go before me.  Eating our heavily truffled omelette was made all the more pleasurable by my act of kindness!

Back at the Coopérative, we also purchased olive oil soap and an olive based foaming bath oil, and, of course, a bottle of the Coopérative rosé wine for lunch (after all they also make wine.)

**The old town of Nyons.**

Nyons Extra Virgin rich yellow olive oil is 'liquid sunshine' and when, after drizzling the oil over fresh salad with or without balsamic vinegar or lemon juice, savouring the aroma and flavour and simply closing ones eyes, one is instantly transported to this beautiful part of Provence.  This oil being low in acidity can be used in cooking, but we usually find that the cheaper Extra virgin oils from the supermarkets are satisfactory for cooking.

Whilst in Nyons, a walk in the old town on market day, coupled with a visit to the lavender distillery and the herb garden, help create the memory of the atmosphere and the Provençal aromas which can be recalled when eating *tapenade* on toast, or olives, or a well oiled hot goats cheese and *lardons* salad, ably assisted, of course, with a good Côtes du Rhône Villages wine. The wine lover should not miss the opportunity while being in the area to visit vignerons in the neighbouring villages of Vinsobres, St. Pantaléon-les-Vignes and Rousset-les-Vignes, all of which produce excellent named Villages wine.

There are many small producers in the area and their oil and olives can be purchased, as with wine, from the producer direct, or from the various weekly markets in Nyons, Vaison-la-Romaine and Carpentras. The choice, especially of olives, is mind blowing!

There are two other areas famed for their olives and oil, the Alpes-Maritime area around Grasse and the Alpilles in the *département* of the Bouche-de-Rhône. Around Grasse the main olive grown is the smaller Cailletier olive which is usually picked when ripe and after steeping in brine produces the only olive that should be used in authentic *'Salade Nicoise.'* These appetising small nutty olives are also used to produce very good quality extra virgin olive oil, not quite as full and slightly more subtle in flavour than Nyons oils. The best oils come from Mougins, and are often medal winners at the Concours Général in Paris. We have found that a visit in February combined with a visit to the *Fête au Citron* in Menton, and possibly if time permits a visit to the exotic Villa Hanbury gardens, located just over the Italian border (don't forget the porcini, parmesan and cheap spirits!) is a welcome diversion in the depths of an English Winter.

In the Alpilles are grown a variety of olives, including the Solonenque and the Picholine, and these are invariably picked when green and unripe to produce a green-yellow grassy, peppery oil, much favoured by the top chefs of Provence for all culinary uses. We believe that the best oil comes from Maussane, but others would say Fontevieille or Mouries. Our suggestion would be taste oil from each village and make one's own choice. The only advice we would give, and we speak from experience, is that as these oils are very popular, and produced in limited quantities, look to purchase early in the year as a mid-Summer visit could be a fruitless, (or should I say oil-less) trip. If the trip does prove fruitless, or in any case, visits to the rocky fortress of Les Baux, with its chequered history, the Moulin de Daudet in Fontvieille, and the Roman antiquities at Glanum on the outskirts of St. Rémy-de-Provence, should be considered.

We hope you have enjoyed our humorous experiences in the pursuit of quality affordable wines and look forward to meeting you one day at the *'Nuit de Vin'* in Rasteau, at a *'Foire'*, a *'Goût'* or at a vigneron's chais, for a memorable tasting, somewhere in deepest France.

# References

1         **Canvas Holidays of Hertford.**

2         **VFB of Cheltenham.**

3         **'Eperon's French Wine Tour' by Arthur Eperon.**

4         **'Arlott on Wine' by John Arlott.**

5         **Roger Harris Wines of Norwich.**

6         **'Terence Conran's France' by Terence Conran.**

7         **'An Englishman in the Midi' by John P Harris.**

8         **'The World Atlas of Wine' by Hugh Johnson.**

9         **'The Wine Buyers Guide' by Robert Parker.**

10        **'Red Wine Guide' by Jim Ainsworth.**